VILLAINS

TRAITORS, TYRANTS, AND THIEVES

By
Richard Platt

Consultant
Robert Fowke

A Dorling Kindersley Book

Dorling **DK** Kindersley
LONDON, NEW YORK, MUNICH,
MELBOURNE, and DELHI

Project Editor Matthew Turner
Project Art Editor Keith Davis
Senior Editor Fran Jones
Senior Art Editor Stefan Podhorodecki
Category Publisher Linda Martin
Managing Art Editor Jacquie Gulliver
Picture Researcher Brenda Clynch
DK Picture Library Jonathan Brooks,
Rose Horridge, Sarah Mills
Production Jenny Jacoby
DTP Designer Siu Yin Ho

First published in Great Britain in 2002 by
Dorling Kindersley Limited
80 Strand, London WC2R 0RL

A Penguin Company

2 4 6 8 10 9 7 5 3 1

The CIP Catalogue record for this book is available
from the British Library

ISBN 0-7513-3919-9

Reproduced by Colourscan, Singapore
Printed and bound by L.E.G.O., Italy

See our complete
catalogue at
www.dk.com

Note to Parents
Every effort has been made to ensure that the information in this book is as up-to-date as possible at the time of
going to press. The internet, by its very nature, is liable to change. Homepage and website content is constantly
being updated, as well as website addresses. In addition, websites may contain material or links to material that may
be unsuitable for children. The publishers, therefore, cannot accept responsibility for any third party websites or any
material contained in or linked to the same or for any consequences arising from use of the internet; nor can the
publishers guarantee that any website or urls featured in this book will be as shown. Parents are strongly advised
to ensure that access to the internet by children is supervised by a responsible adult.

CONTENTS

NTRODUCTION

This book of villains is a catalogue of wickedness. Between the covers you'll find every kind of beastly, vile crook who ever lived. There are the cheats, liars, and forgers, the small-town swindlers, and the scheming, evil kings. Each of them has a gripping tale to tell, and they're all true. Well, almost all.

Sometimes separating fact from fiction is not easy, for you simply can't trust a villain to tell the truth. So lurking between these pages, you may spot a few rogues from the world of story-book and film.

Real or imaginary, all of them have one thing in common. Their bad deeds made them infamous. Between them, they have stolen more money and valuables than you could imagine.

The pirates scoured the salty seas in search of gold. Highwaymen and bad guys of the Wild West rode on

THE NAME SAYS IT ALL – IVAN THE TERRIBLE WAS A 16TH-CENTURY VILLAIN WHO RULED RUSSIA WITH RUTHLESS CRUELTY.

TRIGGER-HAPPY, WILD-WEST
OUTLAWS SHOT FIRST AND
ASKED QUESTIONS LATER.

horseback from misdeed to murder. Gangsters and Mafia mobsters used threats and beatings to get their share. Swindlers and forgers stole so cleverly that their victims hardly noticed they had been cheated. And when they did, it was too late.

Of course, not all villains are thieves. You'll find some brutal killers here, too. And there are traitors who betrayed their friends – or their country. But the biggest villains of all were the least likely to be punished. Cruel, murderous rulers did exactly what they liked – for each time they broke a law they just made a new one! Archvillains usually escaped punishment, too. Although they controlled vast criminal empires, they were so smart that they rarely got caught.

There's space in this book for only a few of the most thrilling tales. For more detail, look for the black Log On "bites" in the book. These will direct you to websites where you can check out more on villains and their wicked world.

Richard Platt

WHAT IS A VILLAIN?

We know they are dangerous and may fear their power, but we still follow their daring adventures. We send the good guys to catch villains – yet secretly admire some of them, and may cheer when they escape. So who are these shadowy figures that we love to hate? And if villains are so wicked, why are they so popular in films and books?

Spot the villain

We can be clear about one thing – villains are bad. But just how bad do you have to be to become a villain? That's not so clear! Murderers like the English poisoner Doctor Crippen are obviously villains, because they plan their crimes, and kill in a calm, pitiless way.

But what about villainy that doesn't leave a

SCREEN VILLAINS OFTEN DRESS IN BLACK TO MAKE THE PLOT EASIER TO FOLLOW. REAL-LIFE VILLAINS ARE SELDOM SO HELPFUL!

bruise or a scar? Thieves may not use violence, but they're still villains to the victims of their crimes.

Just how small can a villain be? Cheating in exams is bad, but does it make you a villain?

N aming villains

So deciding who the villains are is more difficult than it seems. Part of the problem is that we call them by so many different names. They're rogues, scoundrels, and ruffians. They're also known as rascals and badmen, wrongdoers and felons.

In fact, the closer you look, the harder it is to pin a villain down. For only story-book villains or Hollywood bad guys, such as the black-caped Star Wars warrior Darth Vader, are pure, 100 per cent badness.

Most real villains are a sloppy mix of wickedness and bravado, selfishness and greed, cowardice and

WEIRD WORLD

CRIME DOESN'T PAY, AND MOVIE BADDIES CAN'T WIN! HOLLYWOOD RULES PASSED IN 1930 MADE SURE THAT VILLAINS WERE ALWAYS PUNISHED BY THE END OF THE FILM.

daring, cunning and stupidity. There's no single combination – just a million imperfect recipes for evil.

B orn bad?

Maybe instead of lining villains up in an identity parade of wickedness, we should try to find out what makes them bad.

Many take up villainy for the simplest and most selfish of reasons – greed.

THE GLAMOUR OF FILM STARS CAN OBSCURE THE CRUELTY OF THEIR CHARACTERS. HERE ARE FAYE DUNAWAY AND WARREN BEATTY IN A 1967 FILM ABOUT BONNIE AND CLYDE.

9

Many more are just born villains. Growing up in families where crime is a way of life, villainy seems like the only sensible job. In 1920s America, for example, Mafia gangsters taught their children that violence and dishonesty were the fastest ways to gain wealth and power.

Others, such as Australian outlaw Ned Kelly, become villains when they commit a string of small offences, and run away to evade punishment. They soon find that there's no way to return to a normal life. They have nothing to lose by committing more – and greater – crimes.

Cleverness can make people villains, too, for breaking the law is the ultimate challenge. Intelligent villains aim to show the world just how smart they can be. They commit what they believe is the perfect crime, and expect to get away with it.

Which side are you on?

Finally, strongly held political or religious beliefs can turn people into villains. Their enemies call them terrorists, but to their supporters they are freedom fighters.

On the Caribbean island of Cuba, for example, Fidel Castro became a hero when he freed his people from rule by a corrupt leader. However, wealthy Cubans hated the changes he made to their country later,

SECRET AGENTS
LIKE THIS SPY MAY
BE HEROES TO
THE COUNTRY
THEY SERVE, BUT
THEY'RE VILLAINS
TO THOSE WHO
THEY BETRAY.

and many fled to the nearby United States. Nowadays, Castro is loved and loathed in equal measure.

Even the bloodiest of political villains have some friends. Vlad Dracolya – the real-life Count Dracula – was famous for his cruelty. Yet today he is a hero in

The glamorous spy is so likeable that we welcome him or her as a friend – until the "friend" pulls out a gun. The skill of a confidence trickster lies in gaining people's trust, so that nobody

IN OLD-FASHIONED DRAMAS, CHARACTERS LIKE CAPTAIN HOOK PLAY THE VILLAINS WE LOVE TO HATE. WITHOUT THEM, WHO WOULD THE HERO FIGHT?

ONE SMALL MISTAKE CAN MAKE AN HONEST MAN AN OUTLAW

his home country, Walachia (now part of Romania), because he fought against foreign invaders.

D on't be fooled!
Though villainous rulers like these are easy to spot, it is a mistake to imagine that all villains are so obvious. For in certain kinds of villainy, looking and sounding ordinary is an essential skill.

dreams that the trickster is dishonest. We rely on the respectable businessman, but when he vanishes with our life savings, we cry "How could he have done it! He looked just like my dad!"

R ule-breakers
You would think that villains' wicked deeds would make them unpopular, but some become celebrities. Their daring crimes

only from the very rich, and don't use violence. But even brutal robbers like Bonnie and Clyde have become heroes too, because the exciting cat-and-mouse game they play with the police somehow enables us to "forget" they are killers.

Villains of stage and screen
Television dramas and films have helped to turn these villains into heroes. Glamorous stars play their roles, making the villains seem more exciting, more interesting, and more attractive than the good guys and girls. They often dress better, and they seem to have more fun – until they come to a sticky end.

Story-book villains also appear on screen – in police programmes, westerns, and Mafia tales. Hollywood villains wear black, they limp, they have scars, and they're usually obviously cruel and wicked.

The ugly truth
But real life isn't like the movies. Though a handful of true villains, such as Chicago gangster Al Capone, had scars, most don't. And whereas a few live in style, most villains' lives

and sensational escapes make us see them as brave figures who ignore society's rules.

Of course, it's easier to like villains if, like safe-breaker Albert Spaggiari, they steal

are tough, brutal, and short. When the shooting starts, real-life police fire real-life bullets. Dead villains don't get up again to make another movie.

furnace, helps us avoid doing wrong. And would Batman look like such a good guy if he didn't have villains like the Joker to fight?

FOOLISH VILLAINS BELIEVE THEY CAN "GET AWAY WITH MURDER"

Villains have their uses
Wouldn't we all be better off without evil people? Perhaps we would. Life would be a lot safer, for a start. And without daring robbers like Spaggiari, our money would be more secure in banks.

But maybe in a strange way the world needs a few villains. For without a constant reminder of what's bad, it might be more difficult to recognize what's good.

After all, the terrifying figure of the Devil, breathing fire and tossing sinners into a

CONFIDENT THAT THEY WILL ESCAPE, REAL VILLAINS OFTEN TAUNT THE POLICE – JUST AS THE JOKER TEASES BATMAN.

PIRATES BOLD

F or as long as trading ships have put to sea, pirates have followed them, ready to plunder a precious cargo or capture the crew. We may have romantic ideas of daring rascals in eye-patches and earrings, but real pirates were no more than greedy robbers, and many were ruthless killers, too. Villains of the high seas, they got away with murder simply because the law could not reach them.

P irates of old

Nearly 3,000 years ago, pirates pestered the ships of Greece, which controlled the Aegean Sea and much of the Mediterranean Sea. The pirates were an even greater menace in later years when the Roman Empire, based in Italy, ruled the same region. They robbed the ships bringing grain from Egypt. The pirates cruised in galleys – long, speedy ships powered by oars and sails. They hid in creeks and inlets, ready to ambush. The bold pirates rammed their victims' ships before swarming aboard to steal the cargo or capture the crew to sell as slaves.

B ecoming a pirate

The promise of wealth was not the only attraction that drew people into piracy. The life of a sailor in the navy was hard, with low pay, revolting food, and frequent floggings. During wartime, there was the risk of being killed. When a war ended, navies sent many sailors away without pay, and they had to find a new way of making a living. It's easy to see why sailors took up the freer life of piracy. For one thing, many pirate crews got to elect their own captain.

WEIRD WORLD
PORT ROYAL, JAMAICA, WAS A PIRATE TOWN. IN 1692, AN EARTHQUAKE SANK THIS CRIME CAPITAL INTO THE SEA. PEOPLE SAID IT WAS GOD'S JUDGMENT ON A WICKED CITY.

Groaning galleons
In the 16th century, European nations began to conquer the lands of North and South America. Spain seized the richest territories, and her ships sailed back across the Atlantic, their holds groaning with gold and silver. Spanish settlements and treasure galleons were easy targets for pirate ships.

THESE "PASSENGERS" LOOK INNOCENT ENOUGH, BUT THEY'RE REALLY PIRATES IN DISGUISE. ARMED TO THE TEETH, THEY'RE LURING ANOTHER SHIP TO ITS DOOM.

Hero or villain?

The best-known pirate of the time was an Englishman, Sir Francis Drake. He was a privateer, or "official pirate" – someone allowed by his own government to attack foreign ships. In 1577–80 Drake sailed all the way around the world, spending almost six months plundering the Spanish settlements in South America.

Drake sailed home with his ship, the *Golden Hind*, laden with booty. Queen Elizabeth, who took a big share of the loot, was so pleased that she made Drake a knight. In England, Drake was a hero. Yet, to the Spaniards, he was a terrifying villain, a man they called El Draco – "the dragon".

Mighty Morgan

As daring as Drake's cutthroat career was that of Henry Morgan, a Welsh privateer who lived in the following century. Morgan and his men attacked Spanish South America, even burning Panama City to the ground. King Charles II rewarded him with a knighthood and a comfortable position as governor of Jamaica!

BLACKBEARD THE PIRATE WAS A GIANT OF A MAN. HE HAD 14 WIVES, A BELT FULL OF GUNS, AND WAS AFRAID OF NO ONE.

16

Pirate attack

Out at sea, pirates liked to make their victims give up without a fight. This was the purpose of the "Jolly Roger" – the black flag with a skull and crossbones, or some other scary image. They raised it at the start of an attack to strike fear into another crew.

From time to time, however, pirates used a really mean trick. They would raise a friendly flag, not a Jolly Roger. This way, they could sail right up to

but Teach grew an enormous beard that covered his face. For this man was none other than the terrible Blackbeard. He twisted the beard into plaits and tied it with ribbons.

To make himself look even more terrifying, Blackbeard went into battle with lighted "matches" (lengths of cord) stuck under his hat. With a

LOG ON...
www.geocities.com/
captcutlass/page7.html

BLACKBEARD'S FAVOURITE DRINK WAS BRANDY AND GUNPOWDER

PIRATES RAISED THE JOLLY ROGER TO SCARE VICTIMS. SOME FLAGS SHOWED KNIVES, HOURGLASSES, OR BLOOD IN PLACE OF THE SKULL AND CROSSBONES.

naturally wild and fierce look in his eyes, he must have looked like a real devil. Blackbeard even used to frighten his own men, and from time to time he would shoot one of them – just for fun.

an unwary ship. Too late, the crew realized that its visitors were not friends, but pirates.

Blackbeard: terror of the seas

One of the most frightening pirates ever was Edward Teach. In his day men usually shaved,

In November 1718, Blackbeard was killed by Lieutenant Robert Maynard of the British Navy. It took 25 wounds to kill the monstrous pirate, who finally dropped dead in the act of raising his cutlass to kill Maynard. The victorious sailors then chopped his head off and hung it from the bows (front) of their ship.

War on the sea devils

The battle with Blackbeard was part of a major British Navy campaign to stamp out piracy. Between 1716 and 1726, more than 400 pirates were hanged, and many others were killed in sea battles. Two years after killing Blackbeard, the navy caught another pirate ship, off the Bahamas. When the news reached England, it caused a sensation – two of the captured pirates were women!

Warlike women

These captives were the infamous Mary Read and Anne Bonny. Read, from England, had joined both the army and the navy. When pirates seized her ship in the Caribbean, she joined them.

Anne Bonny, from Carolina in America, was married. But she fell in love with a pirate, John "Calico Jack" Rackham, and put on men's clothes to run off to sea with him. Mary and Anne first met on Calico Jack's pirate ship, and they became partners in piracy.

THE NOTORIOUS CAPTAIN WILLIAM KIDD BURIED HIS TREASURE. AFTER HIS EXECUTION IN 1701, MUCH OF IT WAS DUG UP. BUT THERE ARE RUMOURS THAT MORE BOOTY WAITS TO BE FOUND...

ANNE BONNY DRESSED LIKE A MAN AND FOUGHT LIKE A DEVIL. IT WAS NOT UNTIL HER TRIAL THAT HER CREWMATES FOUND OUT SHE WAS A WOMAN!

In battle, Mary and Anne always fought side by side, and were tougher than any man. When the British Navy finally boarded their ship, Mary and Anne bravely fought back, but the male pirates all fled below deck. "Come up and fight like men!," Mary shouted. When nobody replied,

MANY A CAPTURED PIRATE ENDED UP SWINGING FROM THE GIBBET AT EXECUTION DOCK, BY LONDON'S RIVER THAMES.

she fired her pistols into the hold, killing one of the cowardly pirates.

Bad Black Bart

One of the oddest pirates in history was Bartholomew Roberts, a Welshman. Between 1719 and 1722, "Black Bart" Roberts captured more than 400 ships. He roamed the Atlantic Ocean, from the Americas to West Africa.

Black Bart was a very peculiar pirate. Deeply religious, he banned gambling on board his ship, and preferred a nice cup of tea to a bottle of rum. He was tall and dashing, and wore fancy clothes.

Bart was an easy target, and he was eventually shot dead in a sea battle. In 1722, his crew was taken to London, where the biggest-ever pirate trial was held. In all, 74 were found not guilty, two were pardoned, 37 were sent to prison or forced labour, and 52 were hanged.

The trial showed that the world's great trading nations would no longer put up with piracy, and had the power to stop it.

After the execution of Black Bart's men, there were fewer pirate attacks, but piracy did not end. Even now, attacks on ships in the South China Sea and off Africa are common – though the pirates no longer fly the Jolly Roger!

WEIRD WORLD
BOTH BLACK BART AND FRANCIS DRAKE PUT TO SEA WITH ORCHESTRAS. THE MUSICIANS WOULD PLAY TO ENCOURAGE THE MEN IN BATTLE.

STAND AND DELIVER!

Three words terrified travellers in Old England. "Stand and deliver!" was the traditional cry of highwaymen – bandits on horseback who ambushed travellers on lonely roads and moors. They could be violent, killing for just a handful of coins. Hounded by the law, many were hanged for their vicious crimes.

F olk heroes

Highwaymen began to raid England's roads hundreds of years ago, and by the 17th century they were causing serious problems for travellers.

However, ordinary folk rather admired these daring robbers, just as Robin Hood was admired. The longer highwaymen escaped capture, the greater their reputation became. People wrote popular songs about them. If they were caught and tried, crowds often gathered

Nevison's most famous exploit, though, was not a robbery but what he did afterwards. Having held up a man

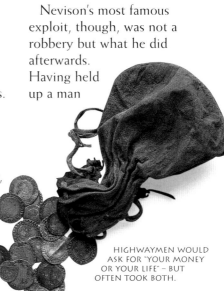

HIGHWAYMEN WOULD ASK FOR "YOUR MONEY OR YOUR LIFE" – BUT OFTEN TOOK BOTH.

HIGHWAYMEN WERE IDEALIZED AS BRAVE "GENTLEMEN ROBBERS"

to cheer them on their way to execution. Sometimes famous women wept at their funerals.

W illiam's wild ride

The greatest of them all was William Nevison (1639–85). He started stealing as a boy, taking his father's money and also his schoolteacher's horse. As a highwayman, William earned a reputation as a "ringleader in rudeness", but he was highly successful.

THE SEDAN CHAIRS WHICH WEALTHY PEOPLE USED FOR SHORT JOURNEYS WERE EASY TARGETS FOR HIGHWAYMEN.

down south in Kent, he devised a cunning alibi – a way to prove he was elsewhere at the time of the crime. In a single day he rode 370 km (230 miles) north to York.

Nevison was arrested for the robbery, but at his trial he called as a witness the Mayor of York, who told the judge that he clearly remembered chatting with Nevison in the city on the day of the crime. Nobody thought it possible to ride such a distance in a single day – a carriage took weeks. As a result, he was released.

21

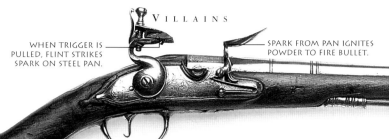

WHEN TRIGGER IS PULLED, FLINT STRIKES SPARK ON STEEL PAN.

SPARK FROM PAN IGNITES POWDER TO FIRE BULLET.

Dick Turpin

This story may have been exaggerated, but it earned Nevison the nickname "Swift Nicks". Today another man, Dick Turpin (1705–39), unfairly takes the credit for the rapid ride. Turpin worked as a butcher, but when his business hit hard times, he began to steal cattle. By the age of 30 he was a highwayman, and two years later a reward of £200 – enough to buy a fine house – was offered for his capture.

Turpin fled and changed his name, but his deeds eventually caught up with him. Arrested on a string of minor offences, he was later identified as the notorious highwayman by his handwriting on a letter he wrote from prison. With nowhere left to run, he was finally hanged in 1739.

Turpin was so famous that even during his lifetime, minstrels praised him in ballads. In 1865 a sad new song boosted his reputation further. The ballad has Turpin, rather than Nevison, riding from London to York. At the end of the song, a tearful Turpin shoots faithful horse Black Bess, rather than let her be captured.

The charming Duval

Ballads like this one suggest that Turpin and other highwaymen were gallant, polite thieves. In reality, most were merely cold-blooded killers. One of the few who deserved a reputation as a gentleman was the French highwayman Claud Duval (1643–70).

Duval became famous when his gang surrounded a coach carrying a gentleman and a

IT WAS THE KILLING OF A NEIGHBOUR'S PRIZE COCKEREL THAT FINALLY LANDED DICK TURPIN IN GAOL.

22

lady on a heath near London.
To show she was
not afraid of the
five masked robbers,
the lady began to play
a flute. Hearing the
tune, Duval pulled from his
saddlebag a similar instrument
and joined in.
At the end, he
invited the
woman to step
from the coach
and dance with
him, which she
duly did.

Duval didn't
let courtesy stand
in the way of
business. After
returning his dancing partner to
the coach, he demanded money
from her husband – but in the
politest possible way.

When this gentleman thief
was finally caught and hanged,
his body was put on display
like that of a prince. Among
the mourners were London's
most fashionable ladies. They
were masked to hide their
identity, but
each sobbed
for the loss
of her hero.

B ad bushrangers

English highwaymen
thrived because the
government
could not afford
to pay for a
police force – and
because law
enforcement was
unpopular among
poor people.

The same
conditions led to
lawlessness in the
18th and 19th centuries in
Australia, where highwaymen
were known as "bushrangers".
Despite the different name,
their business was the same –
robbing travellers.

K elly's gang

Ned Kelly (1855–80) was
Australia's most notorious
bushranger. He led a gang that
not only robbed
travellers, but also

LOG ON...
www.ironoutlaw.com/
html/history_01.html

> ### WEIRD WORLD
> AT HIS HANGING, TURPIN SAT
> ON THE GIBBET WITH THE
> NOOSE SLUNG AROUND HIS
> NECK, CHATTING TO THE
> GUARDS. THEN HE
> BRAVELY LEAPT TO HIS
> DEATH.

HIGHWAYMEN HELD UP VICTIMS WITH
FLINTLOCK PISTOLS LIKE THESE. THE THREAT
OF DEATH WAS USUALLY ENOUGH TO COAX
MONEY AND JEWELS FROM TRAVELLERS.

raided banks and stole horses. Kelly was a superb shot. On one occasion, when a posse of lawmen went out at twilight to capture the gang, he shot two of them dead.

The police caught up with Kelly's gang one winter's night in 1880.

Heavily armed, they surrounded the inn where the gang had taken refuge, and sprayed it with gunfire.

Kelly's last stand

At dawn, Ned emerged from the inn – dressed from the head downwards in iron! He had beaten out a makeshift suit of armour from the blades of ploughs.

EACH OF THE KELLY GANG HAD A £2,000 BOUNTY ON HIS HEAD

Despite his armour, Ned was captured, tried, and sentenced to death. Almost 60,000 people signed a petition begging for mercy, but Kelly was hanged in December 1880.

Australia's poor folk admired the bushranger for fighting the wealthy people who owned all the farms and who exploited the country's landless workers.

Like so many other highwaymen, Ned Kelly lived as an outlaw but died a hero, to be later celebrated in films, art, and literature.

KELLY MADE A LAST STAND AGAINST THE POLICE. MOST OF THEIR BULLETS BOUNCED OFF HIS ARMOUR, BUT HE WAS FINALLY SHOT AND CAPTURED.

AFTER EXECUTION, NED'S HEAD WAS
CUT OFF, SHAVED, AND OILED, AND FIVE
PLASTER "DEATH MASKS" (CASTS) WERE
MADE OF HIS FACE.

THE WILD WEST

Two cowboys face each other in a dusty street. Gunshots ring out and a man falls dead. A gun-slinging villain has killed again! In the lawless American West of the late 19th century, sharp-shooting cowboys fought many such duels. They also killed in ambushes, feuds, battles, and plain murders. Chaos and death followed them whenever they rode out.

IT WAS THE SHERIFF'S JOB TO KEEP LAW AND ORDER IN THE WILD FRONTIER TOWNS, WHERE THE HARSHNESS OF LIFE DROVE DESPERATE MEN TO CRIMINAL ACTS.

Rough justice

It was outlaw gunmen who put the "wild" in the Wild West, the remote plains areas of central North America where people had only recently settled.

These frontier towns were a long way from great cities, the centres of law enforcement. Without lawyers or police, people had to make their own justice. They found that a gun helped settle disputes quickly. Settlers valued bravery and independence, and would fight to the death to defend their homes and property.

Bad beef barons

Violence often flared when settler families challenged rich, powerful ranchers. These "beef barons" grazed cattle on the open, unfenced plains, and tried to drive off settlers who wanted the same land for farms. Hired gunmen protected the big farmers' interests and ruthlessly hunted down those who opposed them.

The killer Kid

Struggles for power between the beef barons also led to fierce battles. In the Lincoln County war of 1878, Billy the Kid (1859/60–81) made his name. "The Kid" had already killed a bully when, at the age of 18, he was hired to protect land owned by a wealthy local rancher. When his boss was

Kid joined a gang who set off to seek revenge.

The "war" went on for almost two years, and at the end of it the Kid was wanted for murder. Though he went on the run, and became the outlaw leader of a cattle-stealing gang, he was eventually tracked down and put on trial. Billy avoided execution by killing two guards and escaping. But his freedom was to be brief.

In July 1881, Sheriff Pat Garrett tracked the Kid down and shot him dead.

Billy the Kid's reputation was fiercer than he deserved. According to legend, he gunned down 21 men – "one for each year he lived". In fact, he probably killed only four.

North vs South

Even four killings seems shocking today, but violence and death were familiar to Billy's fellow Americans, for

WILD-WEST GUNSLINGERS USED SHOTGUNS FOR HOLD-UPS, BUT THEY PREFERRED QUICK-DRAW REVOLVERS IN GUNFIGHTS.

HATRED DROVE JOHN WESLEY HARDIN TO KILL. ODDLY, HIS PARENTS HAD NAMED HIM AFTER JOHN WESLEY, A GENTLE ENGLISH PREACHER OF THE 18TH CENTURY!

they had recently fought a bloody civil war. United as the Confederacy, the Southern states fought the North – the Unionists or "Yankees". The war was over slavery. Southern planters relied on slaves to grow their crops, Unionist states did not want slavery to spread. When Southern states left the Union, war broke out.

Hateful Hardin

The war ended in 1865 with victory for the Union, but many people from the South found it difficult to accept defeat. One of these was John Wesley Hardin (1853–95).

> **WEIRD WORLD**
> KEPT AWAKE BY A MAN SNORING IN THE NEXT HOTEL ROOM, JOHN WESLEY HARDIN FIRED HIS REVOLVER THROUGH THE WALL, KILLING THE NOISY SLEEPER.

Unionist soldiers learned of the murder, but when they came to arrest him, "Wes" killed them all. Friends who shared his hatred for the North helped him conceal the bodies, and Wes went on the run.

HARDIN WAS SHOT IN THE BACK OF THE HEAD IN THE ACME SALOON

Hardin grew up during the Civil War, and came to hate black people and Yankees. When he was only 15 he shot dead a freed black slave who had threatened him during a wrestling match. Three

Over the next few years this outlaw became the most feared gunman in his home state of Texas. He killed at least another 16 men – though he claimed to have shot more than 40.

Dangerous and unpredictable, John Wesley Hardin died just as he had lived – violently. A policeman he had threatened to kill shot him in a bar.

F rank and Jesse James

Like Hardin, the James brothers began their criminal careers at the end of the Civil War. Jesse (1847–82) and Frank (1843–1915) had been members of Confederate gangs raiding Unionists. When peace came, the gangs turned to robbing banks. These crimes made the James brothers popular among ordinary people, who believed that banks used their high interest charges to "rob" customers.

In 1873 the James gang took to holding up trains. Nobody cared as long as they stole cash from the safe, but when they started to rob passengers the gang lost popularity. Public sympathy returned briefly when private detectives hired

LOG ON...
www.crimelibrary.com/
americana/kid/

ORDINARY PEOPLE DIDN'T CARE THAT FRANK AND JESSE JAMES ROBBED TRAIN SAFES. AFTER ALL, IT WASN'T THEIR MONEY!

to catch them tossed a grenade into their house, killing their nine-year-old half-brother. In 1881, after a murderous robbery, the state governor offered a reward of $10,000 for their capture … "dead or alive". To claim it, a gang member shot Jesse in the back of the head while he was dusting a picture frame.

Some of the West's most notorious villains wound up in the Wild Bunch. This was a group of criminals that had formed in 1896 specifically to attack trains. Their leader was cattle thief Butch Cassidy (1866–1909). Outlaws Kid Curry and the Sundance Kid were also members.

The Wild Bunch
Railroads continued to be a tempting target for gunmen long after Jesse James died.

For their headquarters the Wild Bunch chose Hole in the Wall, a grassy canyon in north Wyoming. From there and from other remote hideaways they launched raids on banks, railroads, and ranches.

Train robbers
The Wild Bunch had a dramatic way of robbing trains. First, they stopped the locomotive with a red warning light. Then they ordered the guard to open the express carriage, where money was carried. If he refused, they blew the door off with explosives. More

EVEN IN THE ROLE OF AN OUTLAW, A FILM STAR SUCH AS CLINT EASTWOOD IS ALWAYS THE HERO.

THEY LOOK GRAND, BUT BUTCH CASSIDY (CENTRE) AND THE WILD BUNCH WERE JUST CATTLE RUSTLERS AND TRAIN ROBBERS.

dynamite was used to open the safe. Still more destroyed the bridges behind the train to stop anyone from following them.

Soldiers and lawmen tracked down most of the Bunch, but Butch and Sundance escaped and fled to South America. After a few years of quiet ranching, they took up crime again. Nobody is sure how they died, but the most likely story is that they were ambushed by soldiers in Bolivia in 1909.

Villains into heroes

Gunfighters' lives were usually short and brutal, but their tales made fascinating reading. Less than a year after Billy the Kid's death, for example, authors had written eight novels about him. His killer added a life story, mostly invented, to the list.

It was cheap books like these that helped create the legend of a noble gunfighter-hero fighting for freedom and justice. In truth, many were no more than dangerous, desperate criminals.

THIS IS A REPLICA OF THE COLT .45 REVOLVER USED BY SHERIFF PAT GARRETT TO KILL BILLY THE KID.

GANGSTERS

I'll make you an offer you can't refuse! However big the favour, you always said "Yes" to a Mafia boss. A refusal could mean the end for you – or your family. With threats like this, Chicago's gangsters collected millions of dollars during the early 20th century. They used the money to build the largest network of organized crime in the world.

Organized crime

The Mafia, the mob, the syndicate, the cosa nostra, and the boryokudan are all names meaning more or less one thing – a criminal organization with central control. Using threats and bribery, organized crime gangs befriend people in high places, so that they can walk away free from their terrible crimes.

THE BLACK HAND PRINTED ON A NOTE WARNED PEOPLE TO PAY UP – OR FACE DEATH.

This name also described those who used the hideouts. Mafia groups were bound together by oaths (promises) of loyalty, especially *omertà* – the oath of silence. Mafia members swore not to help the police solve a crime committed by another member. And they always took their own revenge.

The Mafia

The best-known criminal organization, the Mafia, began in Sicily. This island at the toe of boot-shaped Italy has had many rulers, but the Sicilians resisted them. During the

Black-hand gangs

The Mafia gradually became a criminal organization. Mafia gangs got rich by extortion –

SETTLERS FROM SICILY BROUGHT THE MAFIA TO AMERICAN CITIES

9th century many Sicilians fled to the hills to escape the invading Arabs. Their hideouts were called "mafia" by Sicily's new masters.

GANGSTERS COULD LOOK COOL AND MENACING – BUT LIKE MANY WHO LIVE BY THE GUN, THEY ALSO DIED BY THE GUN.

threatening violence if the victim did not pay a bribe. On their notes demanding money they drew symbols of death, such as bloody daggers. And instead of a signature they added a crude picture of a hand. This way of demanding money was nicknamed the "black-hand racket".

Palizzolo. Once in government, he made sure another Mafia don (leader) became the island's prime minister.

Organizations similar to Sicily's crime gangs flourished all over southern Italy. In Naples, for example, many senior members of the army, the police force, and the government belonged to the Camorra. This was a secret society involved in smuggling, road robberies, and other criminal activities.

The mob comes to town

Life in Sicily and southern Italy was hard, and between 1880 and 1920 four million people left to seek a better life in North America. Settling in the cities, the Italians brought with them the rich culture of their homelands. But they also brought the Mafia.

In the United States, the mafiosi (members of the Mafia "families") continued with the black-hand racket. They targeted wealthy Italians and Sicilians in the bustling Italian neighbourhoods that sprang up

WEIRD WORLD

THE WORD "HOOCH" COMES FROM THE NAME OF AN ALASKAN PEOPLE, THE HOOCHINOO, WHO ONCE MADE A DISTILLED DRINK.

Fixing votes

The Mafia gained control of Sicily in 1876 by fixing the elections. At the polls, they threatened to shoot voters who did not elect the Mafia candidate, Don Raffaele

34

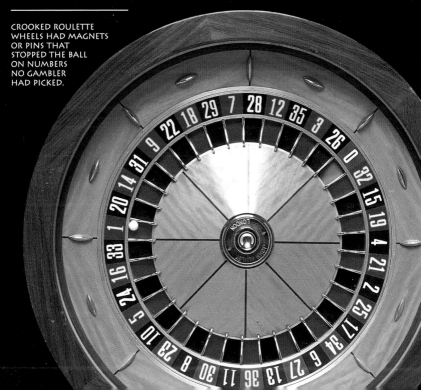

AMERICANS BET CHIPS LIKE THESE IN ILLEGAL GAMBLING DENS RUN BY GANGSTERS. WHEN GAMBLING BECAME LEGAL IN 1931, THE MOB BUILT CASINOS.

in each city. Thanks to *omertà*, there was very little the police could do to stop them.

Bootleg business

In 1919, a new law transformed the Mafia. It ended the black-hand racket almost overnight. It also turned the Mafia from many groups of small-time Little Italy gangsters into one nationwide crime empire.

The law was the National Prohibition Act, which made the brewing and sale of alcoholic drinks illegal. In country areas the law had a lot of support, but city people opposed it.

When the bars closed down, thirsty Americans went looking for a drink. Gangsters were ready to provide it. They were nicknamed "bootleggers" after the heavy drinkers who tucked a bottle into the top of a high boot. The bootleggers supplied

CROOKED ROULETTE WHEELS HAD MAGNETS OR PINS THAT STOPPED THE BALL ON NUMBERS NO GAMBLER HAD PICKED.

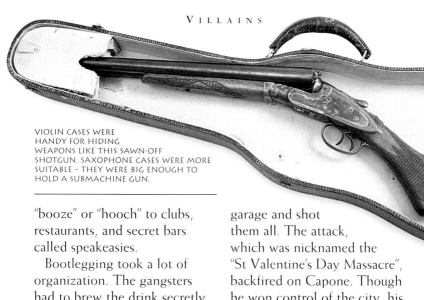

VIOLIN CASES WERE
HANDY FOR HIDING
WEAPONS LIKE THIS SAWN-OFF
SHOTGUN. SAXOPHONE CASES WERE MORE
SUITABLE – THEY WERE BIG ENOUGH TO
HOLD A SUBMACHINE GUN.

"booze" or "hooch" to clubs, restaurants, and secret bars called speakeasies.

Bootlegging took a lot of organization. The gangsters had to brew the drink secretly, or import it from abroad. They had to get it to the speakeasies and, of course, they had to sell it. By the late 1920s, Mafia gangs in different cities had formed links with other gangs who could help them.

Gang warfare

Gangsters who didn't cooperate were killed off by their rivals in gang wars. The most famous of these was between two Chicago gangs run by George "Bugs" Moran (1893–1957) and Al "Scarface" Capone (1899–1947).

By wiping out Moran, Capone hoped to control all Chicago's bootleg liquor. His men disguised themselves as policemen, and on 14 February 1929 they lined up seven unarmed rivals in a back-street

garage and shot them all. The attack, which was nicknamed the "St Valentine's Day Massacre", backfired on Capone. Though he won control of the city, his brutality caused public outrage. He ended up being tried and imprisoned – for not paying his taxes!

MOBSTERS RAN THE "NUMBERS RACKET", IN WHICH PEOPLE BET MONEY ON THE CONTENTS OF THE NEXT DAY'S NEWSPAPERS.

LOG ON...
www.crimelibrary.com/
capone/caponemain.htm

E asy cash

Bootlegging was by far the most profitable of the gangs' illegal trades, but it wasn't the only one. Loan-sharking was a handy sideline. This was a scheme where gangsters lent money at very high rates of interest to people who could not get credit. Fear made customers repay on time, often giving back several times the amount they had borrowed.

Gangsters also ran the "numbers rackets". These were like lotteries, in which gamblers bet money trying to guess a particular number that would be printed in the next day's newspaper – such as the total sum of money traded in the financial district. Those who guessed right won money. Gamblers liked to play, as they knew the gangsters could not predict the number and fix the outcome.

WEIRD WORLD
AFTER SHOOTING A RIVAL, AL "SCARFACE" CAPONE TOLD POLICE THE DEAD MAN "...WAS A GRAND GUY. WE BOTH LOVED THE OPERA."

L et's do business!

Surprisingly, much of the gangsters' money came from ordinary businesses, such as companies that collected rubbish or sold food to restaurants. The gangsters used terror to make sure that customers traded only with companies owned by other gang members, so competitors soon went out of

AL CAPONE WAS A RUTHLESS, COLD-BLOODED KILLER WHO EVEN SHOT HIS FRIENDS IF THEY STOOD IN HIS WAY.

business. Gangsters used violence to take over trade unions – societies that fought for workers' rights – and stole the union funds.

Murder, Inc.

Violence also kept the whole crime organization running smoothly. Those who stepped out of line could expect a visit from "Murder, Inc." – a branch of the organized crime network that dealt out death and injury. Gang leaders who wanted someone killed or badly hurt would pay Murder, Inc.'s Louis Buchalter (1897–1944)

and Albert Anastasia (1902–57) to execute or wound the victim, or to send a "hit man" to do it.

Public concern about the rise in organized crime helped end prohibition in 1933 – but the criminal organizations survived.

Today's gangsters sell heroin instead of hooch, and they no longer talk with a Sicilian accent. For organized crime has now spread worldwide.

Big in Japan

In Japan, for example, gangsters are called yakuza, a word meaning "good for nothing". The yakuza belong to the boryokudan, or "tough gangs", which began in the 16th

CHICAGO GANGSTERS BOUGHT MACHINE GUNS FROM THE US ARMY AND USED THEM TO SPRAY RIVALS WITH BULLETS.

century. Today there are more than 2,000 gangs in Japan, controlled by a few "super-gangs". One of the most

Mafia – gambling, drugs, murder, and extortion. Japanese police estimate that yakuza hit-men carry out a third of all

WHOLE-BODY TATTOOS ARE THE YAKUZA GANGSTERS' UNIFORM

powerful is the Yamaguchi-gumi, formed by Kazuo Taoka, Japan's own Al Capone, after World War II (1939–45).

S harp dressers

Yakuza used to wear traditional Japanese clothes and carry swords, as a reminder that their gangs were once made up of rebel samurai (warriors). Now they copy the American Mafia and prefer to wear western clothes and sunglasses. The whole-body tattoos hidden under their sharp suits are a sign of bravery, for even small tattoos are very painful.

Japan's yakuza are involved in similar enterprises to the US

murders in the country. Like organized criminals everywhere, the yakuza have so many powerful friends that it is hard to stop their vast empire from growing.

GANGS OF REBEL SAMURAI WARRIORS CALLED *MACHI-YAKKO* SET THE SCENE FOR THE YAKUZA MOBSTERS OF TODAY.

MURDER MOST FOUL

Murder stories are gruesome to read, but strangely hard to resist. They are fascinating because it's so hard to understand what drives people to kill. Taking someone's life is a special, horrible kind of crime, with special, horrible punishments. So what is it that turns ordinary people into killers?

A mind to kill

Some people kill for money – they do not have enough, or the victim has more. People can become murderers if their mind does not work in the way that it should and they cannot tell right from wrong. And strongly held political or religious beliefs can be enough to make people think that their victim is evil and deserves to die.

Those who kill for their political beliefs are called "assassins". This word comes from the Arabic language. Later, English-speaking people borrowed the word to describe anyone who kills for political reasons, especially if their murder is so reckless that they are unlikely to escape

FOR A HIT-MAN OR AN ASSASSIN, KILLING IS AS EASY AS SQUEEZING A TRIGGER. BUT COLD-BLOODED MURDER IS AN AWFUL CRIME, WITH TERRIBLE CONSEQUENCES.

punishment. This is especially true of assassins who kill national leaders.

Avenging the South

When actor John Wilkes Booth (1839–65) assassinated American president Abraham Lincoln in 1865 he didn't expect to escape, but he didn't care. Booth was a fanatical supporter of the Southern states that had lost the Civil War (1861–65). This war had been fought over slavery. A racist, Booth was enraged when Lincoln suggested that freed black slaves might vote in elections.

Booth rode his horse to the Washington's Ford Theatre, where Lincoln was watching a comedy. Booth walked into the president's box, drew a small pistol, and shot the president in the head. Then he leaped onto the stage shouting "Sic semper tyrannis!" – Latin for "Thus ever to tyrants!" The jump broke his leg, but he limped to the stage door, mounted his horse, and escaped. Lincoln died in the morning. His killer didn't live much longer. He was caught 12 days later and shot.

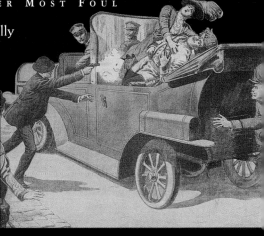

SERBIAN STUDENT GAVRILO PRINCIP KILLED JUST TWO PEOPLE, BUT THE ASSASSINATION STARTED A WAR IN WHICH MILLIONS DIED.

Booth may have actually made things worse for the cause he supported. Northerners used the assassination as an excuse for bad treatment of the defeated Southerners. But another assassination half a century later was to have far worse consequences.

A murder that started a war

Europe was in turmoil in 1914, as the continent's many different nationalities jostled for power. Serbian people wanted to expand their country by uniting with neighbouring nations which were then part of the huge Austro-Hungarian empire.

Bosnian Serb Gavrilo Princip (1894–1918) believed assassination could help achieve this aim. He was a

41

member of an activist group called "Young Bosnia". The activists found out that the future emperor of Austria-Hungary, the Archduke Ferdinand, would be visiting the city of Sarajevo in Bosnia. Princip and five others went to kill him.

The road to ruin

On the morning of 28 June, one of the group hurled a bomb at the archduke's car. It bounced off, but the explosion injured passers-by and hurt an official in the car behind. The archduke was unharmed, and went ahead with a mayor's reception at the city hall.

Afterwards, the archduke decided to visit the injured official in hospital. On the way, his driver took the wrong turning and stopped the car. Unfortunately he stopped directly in front of Moritz Schiller's store, where Princip was buying a sandwich. The Serbian pulled out a pistol, took aim, and pulled the trigger.

The assassination upset the delicate balance of European politics, tipping the continent into World War I. By its end, four years later, more than 20 million people had died.

Bungling killers

Not all assassins have as much "luck" as Princip. Indeed, some have no luck at all. Ask Cuba's leader, Fidel

MEDICAL STUDENTS PAID GOOD MONEY FOR BODIES, SO BURKE AND HARE BECAME MURDERERS TO SUPPLY THEM.

Castro (b.1926/7), who has survived more than 600 attempts on his life. In 1964–65 alone, America's Central Intelligence Agency (CIA) sent spies 30 times to kill him.

The CIA tried everything – an exploding cigar, poisonous milk shakes, a wetsuit dusted with nerve poison, and deadly thallium powder sprinkled in his shoes when he put them outside a hotel door to be cleaned. All their attempts failed. Castro even outwitted Mafia mobsters hired by the CIA to shoot him.

Life is cheap

Assassins believe that the cause they are fighting for is more important than the life they are taking. Other killers commit their crimes for less noble reasons, such as money. In 19th-century Scotland a life was worth just £10. This was the amount that surgeon Robert Knox paid two Irish murderers, William Burke (1792–1829) and William Hare (1790–1860), for the bodies of their victims. Knox needed corpses to dissect (cut up) in his lectures at Edinburgh's medical school. Executed

THE GRAVEYARDS OF EDINBURGH HAD WATCHTOWERS TO LOOK OUT FOR GRAVE ROBBERS.

MEDICAL SCHOOLS NEEDED FRESH CORPSES
SO THAT STUDENTS COULD WATCH EXPERT
SURGEONS SHOW OFF THEIR SKILLS.

any more. It was an invitation to murder, and Burke and Hare greedily accepted.

Over the next few months the pair killed at least 15 more people, suffocating them so that there were no signs of violence. They were discovered only when they held a party in a room where one of their victims lay dead under a pile of straw. A lodger found the body and raised the alarm.

At the trial that followed, Hare saved his neck by giving evidence. Found guilty of murder, Burke was hanged in 1829. His body was immediately used in an anatomy lecture.

criminals were sent for dissection, but Knox needed more specimens. To make up the shortage, he bought the bodies from grave robbers – villains who dug up the recently buried.

Grim trade

Burke and Hare pretended to be grave robbers when one of Hare's lodgers died. The two men carried his body to Knox. The surgeon checked it was fresh, paid them, and told them to come back if they got

Demon barber

The grisly work of Burke and Hare made them legends – just like the murderous 19th-century London barber, Sweeney Todd.

When customers visited his Fleet Street shop for a shave, Sweeney Todd made sure that his razor was especially sharp.

NOBODY IN LONDON GAVE A
CLOSER SHAVE THAN
SWEENEY TODD, THE
MURDEROUS
BARBER.

SWEENEY TODD
THE DEMON
BARBER

MELLFONT
PRESS

With a quick
slash, he cut their
throats, then pushed a
secret lever to tip them
through a hidden trapdoor
in the floor. Todd cut up
the body in the basement,
and sold the meat to a
nearby pie shop.

This meat-pie
murderer would be one
of the world's worst
villains … if the story
were true. But it's not.
Sweeney Todd was
invented to boost the
sales of one of the
trashy magazines that
flourished in London
at that time.

Terrible but true
Truth is, however,
stranger than fiction. In a real-life
murder story from 19th-century
America, a killer really did use
secret trapdoors and hidden
chutes to tip victims to
their deaths.

His name was
Herman Webster
Mudgett (1860–96).
Or at least, that was

NEXT TIME YOU EAT A
MEAT PIE, FIRST TAKE A
REALLY CLOSE LOOK AT
THE JUICY PIECES …

45

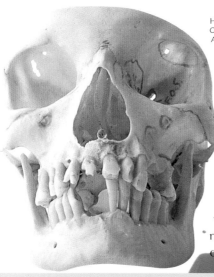

HOLMES USED VILE METHODS TO DISPOSE OF HIS VICTIMS. SOME HE THREW INTO AN ACID BATH TO REDUCE THEIR BODIES TO BLEACHED WHITE SKULLS AND BONES.

By 1896, Mudgett was living in Chicago where he got a job in a chemist's shop. When the lady owner mysteriously disappeared, Holmes took over the business. Later he moved it across the road into a house which he'd had built. Vast and rambling, the building was full of deadly secrets.

H.H. HOLMES TOLD HIS LAWYER THAT HE HAD KILLED 133 PEOPLE

one of them. He had changed it to Harry Howard Holmes by the time he was kicked out of a Michigan medical school for stealing corpses.

Blood money

The bodies were intended for dissection, but Mudgett wanted them for deception. He took out insurance policies on imaginary family members. After faking their "accidental deaths" using the stolen corpses, he claimed the insurance money. Like Burke and Hare, however, Herman Mudgett did not stop at borrowing corpses.

Murder Castle

In some rooms, doors opened onto brick walls or steep drops. In others, greased chutes connected the second-floor rooms to the basement. This contained acid baths for dissolving human flesh, a dissecting table, and a furnace for burning bodies.

Here, in what the newspapers would later nickname "Murder Castle", H.H. Holmes killed and dismembered at least 27 people, and possibly many more. Holmes was finally caught for killing his partner (in yet another insurance swindle) and hanged.

Holmes was what we now call a serial killer – someone who murders again and again. In August 1888, while the skeletons were piling up in his grisly mansion, another serial killer was stalking the foggy streets of London.

London's first serial killer

He preyed on women from Whitechapel, then a poor part of London. He always killed in the same way, by cutting victims' throats with a long knife before skilfully slicing up their bodies. The horrid care with which he did this earned him the nickname "Jack the Ripper". It also led to whispers that he was a respectable surgeon.

Jack killed seven times, spreading terror through London. In November the killings stopped as suddenly as they had started. Jack's identity is still a mystery, for the murderer was never caught.

Jack the Ripper's bloody crimes were a very public way of showing how much he hated women. Most murderers, though, want to hide their crimes. Dr Hawley Crippen (1862–1910) did this so cleverly that he thought he'd get away with murder.

The case of Crippen

An American medical man, Crippen moved to London with Belle, his second wife. When

LOG ON...
http://ccbit.cs.umass.edu/lizzie/

LONDONERS WERE USED TO READING ABOUT BLOODY MURDERS, BUT JACK THE RIPPER'S BRUTALLY SKILFUL KILLING SHOCKED THEM.

47

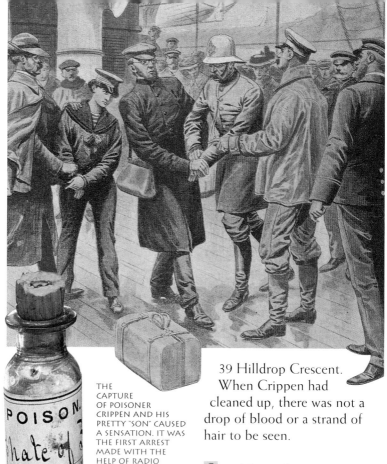

THE CAPTURE OF POISONER CRIPPEN AND HIS PRETTY "SON" CAUSED A SENSATION. IT WAS THE FIRST ARREST MADE WITH THE HELP OF RADIO TRANSMISSIONS.

he lost his well-paid job, their relationship soured, and eventually each partner was unfaithful. Hawley's sweetheart was his secretary, Ethel le Neve.

By 1910 Crippen was getting tired of Belle. He poisoned her, cut her body into pieces, and carefully buried them in the cellar of their home at 39 Hilldrop Crescent. When Crippen had cleaned up, there was not a drop of blood or a strand of hair to be seen.

Suspicious circumstances
Crippen told everyone that Belle had returned to America. Soon afterwards, he claimed, she died suddenly. But when Ethel started wearing Belle's jewels, friends grew suspicious and went to the police.

They believed Crippen's tale – until he and Ethel left their jobs to take an "extended trip". Detectives took a closer look at 39 Hilldrop Crescent. Loose bricks in the cellar floor led them to what was left of Belle.

The murder story, complete with pictures of Crippen and le Neve, appeared in the newspapers just as the pair boarded the steamship *Montrose*. Ethel was dressed as Crippen's "son", and the pair thought they were safe once at sea.

WEIRD WORLD
HARRY HOWARD HOLMES WAS VERY PARTICULAR ABOUT HIS BURIAL. HE LEFT STRICT INSTRUCTIONS FOR A CONCRETE-FILLED COFFIN AND A GRAVE 3 M (10 FT) DEEP.

C aught by radio
However, their disguise was poor, and they had not taken into account a new invention: radio. The ship was one of the first to have a transmitter, and the sharp-eyed captain used it to send this message:

"Have strong suspicion that Crippen London cellar murderer and accomplice are among saloon passengers. Moustache taken off – growing beard – accomplice dressed as boy."

As the *Montrose* steamed towards Canada, police pounced on the pair. At Crippen's trial the evidence persuaded the jury that he had indeed killed Belle, and the deadly doctor was executed on 23 November 1910.

EVERYONE THOUGHT LIZZIE HAD KILLED HER PARENTS, BUT NOBODY COULD PROVE IT.

S cot free
Not all trials end with conviction. After one notable trial, the prime suspect walked free.

Lizzie Borden (1860–1927) lived with her father and stepmother in Fall River, Massachusetts, USA. She claimed to have found their bodies at home on 4 August 1892. They had been beaten to death with a sharp weapon, though this was never found.

Suspicion fell on Lizzie from the start. She had often argued about money with her parents, and had tried to buy poison the previous day. Even the local children taunted her with a cruel new skipping rhyme:

Lizzie Borden took an axe
And gave her mother forty whacks;
And when she saw what she had done,
She gave her father forty-one.

Lizzie lived on in Fall River until her dying day. There was too little evidence to convict her, but the locals never once doubted her guilt.

49

STOP, THIEF!

Rob a few coins from a pocket, and everyone will call you a petty thief. But steal millions from a top-security bank vault, and you are considered a criminal genius. Although no one likes a common pickpocket, we seem to have a soft spot for plucky rogues who use their wits and dare to attempt the impossible crime.

Bold Blood

One man who really took a risk was Irishman Colonel Thomas Blood (c1618–80). He dazzled English people, and their king, by the sheer nerve of his crime. In 1671 Blood stole the Crown Jewels – the gold ornaments used by England's kings and queens on special occasions.

A DARING SAFE-CRACKER MAY HAVE MANY CLEVER SKILLS, BUT HE IS STILL A THIEF.

The jewels were kept in the Tower of London. Blood's cunning first step was to make friends with the Keeper of the Jewels who guarded them when they were on show to visitors. Blood asked his new friend to open the Jewel room early one morning so he and some friends could have a private viewing. Once the door was unlocked, Blood and his henchmen beat the keeper with a mallet and stole the jewels.

Their plan would have succeeded, if the keeper had not recovered and alerted the tower guards. Arrested as he fled, Blood handed over the crown, which he had flattened with the mallet in order to hide it under his coat. Curiously, Blood was never punished. King Charles II interviewed him in private, then awarded Blood a pension for his villainy!

The great escape artist

Blood's talk may have saved his neck, but other thieves relied on strength, agility, or brains. Jack Sheppard (1702–24) used all of these in a series of escapes that made him England's most wanted man.

Trained as a carpenter, Jack found he could make a better living by thieving from the houses where he worked. Caught and sent to prison for stealing early in 1724, he escaped not once, but four times in a row.

> **WEIRD WORLD**
> TO GAIN THE TRUST OF THE KEEPER OF THE JEWELS, BLOOD DISGUISED HIMSELF AS A VICAR, AND PROPOSED THAT THE KEEPER'S SON MARRY HIS (IMAGINARY) DAUGHTER.

It was Jack's final, sensational escape, from the strongest cell of London's most secure prison, that ensured his fame. From a bent nail he made a key to unlock his leg irons. Breaking through seven locked doors, he climbed to the roof then lowered himself to the ground on a blanket rope.

Foolishly, Jack strutted around London drinking and bragging, and he was easily arrested yet again. A crowd of 200,000 turned out to watch his execution. His career as London's greatest escaper had lasted less than a year.

WITHOUT THE JEWELS THAT BLOOD PLANNED TO STEAL, ENGLAND'S KINGS AND QUEENS COULD NOT BE PROPERLY CROWNED.

Dillinger mixed with bank robbers and learned their trade. When he was released, in May 1933, he committed a series of armed robberies. The police caught him in September, but Dillinger was rescued – by a gang who had themselves just escaped from gaol. Dillinger joined them, and together they carried out a series of outrageous robberies. They even raided police armouries (gun stores) to steal machine guns and bulletproof vests!

BANK ROBBER JOHN DILLINGER USED THIS HAND-CARVED WOODEN GUN TO HELP HIM ESCAPE FROM PRISON.

Their luck didn't last, though, and by January 1934 Dillinger was again behind bars. This time he was put in a gaol that was supposed to be "escape

IN 10 MONTHS, DILLINGER AND HIS GANG KILLED 10 MEN

Public enemy No. 1
John Dillinger (1903–34), one of America's most notorious robbers, was also famous for his many escapes from prison.

His short life of crime started when, as a 20-year-old, he stole a car. Soon after this he was caught mugging a grocer and sentenced to a minimum of 10 years in prison. It turned out to be a villains' training school!

proof". By March, Dillinger had proved it was not. He carved a gun from wood and used it to force a gaoler to unlock his cell. He brazenly drove to freedom in a sheriff's car.

Shopped to the cops
Dillinger returned to bank robbery, but the police were closing in. In April they surrounded a hotel where he

was hiding, but he slipped away when the shooting started. Finally, an informer told the police that Dillinger would be going to see a film in Chicago on Sunday, 22 July. Police closed in as he left the cinema, and shot the robber dead when he reached for his gun.

S mall-time thieves

It was Dillinger's daring, and the sums he stole, that made his name. However, it wasn't necessary to steal a fortune to become a criminal celebrity.

LOG ON...
www.historybuff.com/
library/refbonnie.html

Bonnie and Clyde never stole more than $1,500 in a single raid, yet millions of newspaper readers followed their crime spree through to its tragic end.

Bonnie Parker (1911–34) met Clyde Barrow (1909–34) shortly before he was arrested for burglary. When he was released from prison after 20 months, they met up again and began a series of robberies.

The pair targeted restaurants, petrol stations, and banks. They shot anyone who stood

BONNIE AND CLYDE LOVED POSING WITH THEIR GUNS. AFTER KILLING THE CRIME COUPLE, POLICE FOUND 14 GUNS AND 3,000 BULLETS IN THEIR CAR.

THE "SEWER RATS" LEFT BEHIND VALUABLES, BECAUSE THEY HAD ALL THE GOLD BARS THEY COULD CARRY.

It stood for Albert Spaggiari (born 1932). This ingenious thief lived near Nice, a fashionable resort on France's southern coast. Spaggiari found out that the city's sewers ran close to a big bank. By digging just 7.5 m (8 yd) from the sewer, he guessed he could tunnel into the bank's vault (underground safe).

Inside the bank, the vault was protected by a steel door that was 1 m (3 ft 3 in) thick. Even a thief armed with dynamite could not open it.

up to them, and as the trail of dead policemen grew longer, the pressure to stop them got stronger. In April 1934 the two were traced to Louisiana. The following month police laid a roadside trap. When Bonnie and Clyde drove past, sharp-shooters sprayed their car with a hail of deadly bullets.

Bonnie and Clyde would have lived to rob again if a "friend" had not told police

ONE ROBBER WAS CAUGHT WHEN HE TRIED TO SELL A GOLD BAR

where to find them. And without another helpful "friend" French police might still be looking for the gang that carried out the "Crime of the 20th Century" in 1976.

The sewer rat of Nice
The informer in question gave the police a list of initials. The first on the list was "A.S.".

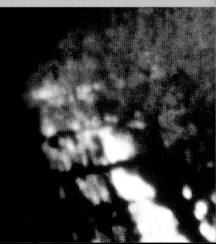

But Spaggiari did not have to. In fact, when he and his gang tunnelled into the vault over a mid-July weekend in 1976, they welded the door shut. This made sure that they could not be disturbed as they looted as much as $20 million in gold bars, banknotes, and valuables.

By the time bank staff tried to open the safe on Monday morning, the gang had disappeared, leaving no fingerprints, and few clues. Police were baffled – until they got the tip-off that led them to Albert Spaggiari.

They arrested him, but Spaggiari escaped by leaping from a second-floor window (a parked car cushioned his fall). He sped away on a waiting motorcycle and has not been seen since. Only a tiny fraction of the stolen wealth has been recovered.

SEWER PIPES LED SPAGGIARI'S GANG TO A BIGGER TUNNEL, WHERE A GETAWAY CAR WAS AWAITING THEM.

WEIRD WORLD
ALBERT SPAGGIARI'S FREEDOM LEAP CRUSHED THE CAR ROOF HE LANDED ON – SO HE POSTED THE OWNER ENOUGH MONEY TO REPAIR IT.

SWINDLERS

Psst! Do you want to buy the Statue of Liberty? Or the Eiffel Tower? Most people know they are not for sale, but that doesn't stop cheats and swindlers. They offer the greedy and unwary deals that seem too good to be true, such as a chance to buy a famous landmark, or a bet on a horse that's sure to win.

Confidence tricksters

The first step of a swindler is to gain a victim's trust or confidence, which is why these villains are known as "confidence tricksters", or "con men". Many con men start out as card-sharps (card cheats). Their simplest swindle is a street-corner game called "chase-the-lady". Players bet on which of three cards is the queen. They double their money if they win.

It seems easy, especially when bystanders see the

THE MAN WHO SOLD THE STATUE OF LIBERTY – AND THE BROOKLYN BRIDGE – MAY BE NOTHING MORE THAN A NEW YORK LEGEND.

again. What they don't know is that the people winning are all friends of the dealer. The cheat cunningly switches the cards when *real* gamblers join in the game.

Canada Bill

The finest card-sharp ever was "Canada" Bill Jones. Born in a gypsy tent in England, Bill got his nickname after learning his skills from a Canadian card-sharp. By the time he moved south to cheat Americans, Bill was a professional gambler.

Canada Bill enjoyed some natural advantages. He had a stupid grin, and his shuffling way of walking made him look like a loser. The foolish

questions he asked also helped persuade people that they could easily take some money off him in a quick card game. It always turned out to be an expensive mistake.

Smart city people usually knew better than to bet on chase-the-lady. So like other card-sharps, Canada Bill preyed on "rubes" (innocent country folk). Through the 1850s and 1860s he swindled thousands of people on river-boats and trains, and at race-tracks.

Bill fooled them with a trick no other sharp could repeat. While throwing the

CROOKED DEALERS SECRETLY SWAP CARDS WHILE GAMBLERS REACH FOR THEIR WALLETS.

cards down, he could hide the winning card, putting a worthless one in its place.

When Bill couldn't talk people into a game, he tempted them with impossible bargains. He rented an "Everything-for-a-Dollar" shop and filled its front with luxuries worth much more. Nobody bought them. Everyone who entered got drawn into a game of chase-the-lady in a back room. They always left the shop penniless.

IN *THE STING*, THE HOLLYWOOD VERSION OF WEIL'S HORSE-RACING TRICK, ROBERT REDFORD PLAYS A CON MAN.

Crooked cons

Bill's victims knew they were taking a gamble, but con men can persuade people that they are certain to make money. They encourage their victims' greed, promising huge profits in return for a small payment. Often they make a deal sound slightly illegal to discourage the victim from going to the police when they lose.

The big sting

American con man Joseph Weil (1875?–1976) invented some of the best "big cons" – tricks that fleece a victim of all his money. The 1973 film *The Sting* tells the story of a big con, in the form of a clever gambling fraud.

A con man tells a "mark" (an intended victim) that he has a deal with a dishonest telegraph operator (someone who sends messages by an old-fashioned version of the telephone). This man secretly tells the con man which horse has won as soon as he gets the track results. Only after the mark has bet on the winner does the operator send the results to the betting shops.

After winning small sums, the mark is convinced he cannot lose, and wagers a huge sum –

in a bogus betting shop where the clock is 10 minutes slow. Thanks to a "misunderstanding", he backs the wrong horse.

Dog-gone nerve

"Short cons" (simpler tricks) worked just as well. In one old favourite, Weil went into a bar with a dog on a lead. Chatting to the barman, he praised the dog as a rare and valuable breed, and explained how much his furry friend meant to him. Finishing his drink, he revealed

payment to pass on to the owner.

Later, Weil returned, and "reluctantly" sold the dog to the barman for $200. Convinced that he could sell it on for $300, the barman went in search of the stranger – without success. The address did not exist. The stranger, of course, was Weil's friend and helper, and the dog was a worthless mutt.

LOG ON...
hoaxes.com/graham.html
www.museumof

WEIL SET UP A GAMBLERS' BANK THAT RAKED IN $480,000 A YEAR

that he had to go to a meeting, and asked if he might leave the dog in the bar for several hours. The barman readily agreed.

While Weil was gone, another man came into the bar and immediately raved about the dog. "I have to have it!" he cried, and offered the barman $300. Of course the barman couldn't sell the dog, but he took the stranger's address, and a $50 advance

Postage scamp

Like Joseph Weil's "certain bet", Charles Ponzi's 1920 money-making scheme seemed to offer big profits without risk. Italian-born Ponzi (c.1882–1949) had settled in Massachusetts in the USA. He bragged that he had

ONLY GREEDY AND DISHONEST PEOPLE FELL FOR THE "PRICELESS DOG" TRICK. THEY WOULD END UP PAYING A SMALL FORTUNE FOR A WORTHLESS MONGREL.

59

CHARLES PONZI SWINDLED AMERICANS OUT OF $15 MILLION AT A TIME WHEN A TEACHER EARNED JUST $1,000 A YEAR.

people were suspicious. But when he paid the first investors as promised, there was a rush to join the scheme, and thousands sent in their money.

Collapse!
But Ponzi was not investing the money. Instead, he used the money sent by later investors to pay the "profits" of the people who had first joined. The scheme collapsed as soon as the flow of money slowed, and the fraudster was jailed.

found a loophole in the international postage system. When people ordered goods from abroad, they could pay for the return postage with coupons. But changes in the value of money in different countries

PONZI'S SCHEME CAUSED THE COLLAPSE OF SIX BANKS

meant that a coupon bought for a cent in Spain, for example, paid for six cents' worth of stamps in the USA.

Promises, promises
Ponzi offered to invest people's money in the coupons. He promised to give them back their money, plus half as much again, after 45 days. At first,

Today, similar get-rich-quick frauds are called "Ponzi schemes" after their inventor. They are also called "pyramid schemes" because each layer of a pyramid needs many times more blocks than the layer above. When the blocks run out, the pyramid collapses.

Quack cures

Weil and Ponzi offered wealth, but quack doctors promise health. These con men are nicknamed for the "quacking" (loud boasting) that they use to sell worthless remedies.

NO ONE KNOWS IF MODERN "CURES", SUCH AS CRYSTALS, ACTUALLY WORK, BUT PEOPLE STILL BUY THEM.

Many quacks are at work today, but none has matched the success of Scotsman James Graham (1745–94). This crook played on the novelty of electricity, which had been recently discovered and was not really understood.

In 1780 Graham opened his "Temple of Health" in London. He gave grand lectures, during which the audience received a small electric shock from their wired-up seats.

Graham's real source of income was individual treatment. London's most fashionable people (including England's future king, George IV) queued for Graham's cures. He gave them "electrical baths", sat them on his "magnetic throne", or buried them up to their necks in soil. The fees he charged for such treatments were often more than ordinary people earned in a whole year.

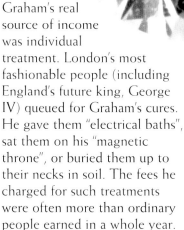

Graham's business thrived for three or four years, but he eventually fell victim to his own crank ideas. In 1793 he gave up eating, dressed himself in a suit of turf, and tried to stay alive by rubbing his arms and legs with Ethereal Balsam – a remedy he had invented. He died soon after.

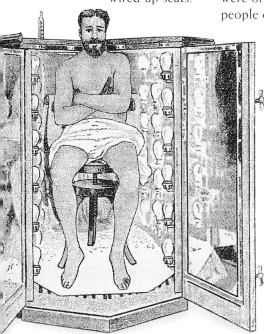

BOGUS 19TH-CENTURY DOCTORS SUGGESTED THAT ELECTRICAL TREATMENTS, LIKE THIS "LIGHT BATH", CURED ALL MANNER OF DISEASES.

IT'S A FAKE!

Wouldn't it be great if you could just print as much money as you could ever spend? This is exactly what some forgers do – until they get caught and sent to prison. Making copies of other valuable items, such as jewellery or paintings, is less risky and just as profitable. And for scientific fakers, money doesn't seem to matter – it's the fame and glory that they crave.

Making a mint
Forged coins are as old as cash itself. Before paper currency was first used in 17th-century Europe, coins were made of precious metals such as gold. Forgers fooled the unwary by making copies of coins from cheap metal, and then coating them in a thin layer of gold.

FORGERS BLEACH US $1 BILLS AND PRINT $50 NOTES ON THEM

Printing fake banknotes used to be much easier than today. In the past, private banks could

PRINTING PILES OF MONEY WOULD BE HANDY – BUT IT'S DIFFICULT, COSTLY, AND TOTALLY ILLEGAL!

issue their own banknotes, and so many designs were issued that not even bank staff knew them all. During the American Civil War (1861–65), 1,600 banks printed a total of 7,000 designs. Forgers joined them, printing so many fakes that half of all the money circulating was counterfeit (forged).

Today, countries have a single currency, with notes in just a few values. Banknotes also include features that are difficult to copy, such as holograms, metal threads, and watermarks – pictures or patterns that appear when you hold the money up to the light.

Cash for questions

The villains behind forgeries are not all inky-fingered printers. Some are slick-suited executives, for faking can make money in almost any kind of business – even television. If a TV show isn't popular enough, a little trickery sometimes helps boost the viewing figures.

In a series of nail-biting episodes of the 1950s American quiz show *Twenty One*, for example, contestant Charles van Doren seemed to have an uncanny knack of getting the right answers again and again.

DESTINED FOR DESTRUCTION, THESE FORGED WRISTWATCHES ARE HARD TO TELL FROM THE COSTLY BRANDS THEY IMITATE.

Millions of viewers tuned in, and Van Doren became famous. Then in 1957 the truth leaked out – to boost their ratings, the show's producers had been giving him the answers.

Viewers felt betrayed, and the government investigated the scandal. Asked why he did it, Van Doren, a university professor, said he thought that by winning he could make viewers value education.

Master faker

Another forger who claimed he didn't do it for the money was the Dutch painter Han van Meegeren (1889–1947), who faked the work of famous 17th-century artists. His excuse was that he did it to get his revenge on critics who didn't like his original modern paintings.

Van Meegeren expertly copied the great Dutch artist Johannes Vermeer and sold the "masterpieces" for huge sums. When arrested, he claimed to have painted five more "Vermeers". Art experts did not believe him – until he painted another before their very eyes.

Van Meegeren was a clever faker. He knew scientists would test the age of the canvas of his forgeries. So he bought genuine 17th-century paintings, scraped off the pictures, and painted new ones – using paint made from old colours.

THE 1994 FILM *QUIZ SHOW* STARRED RALPH FIENNES AS CHARLES VAN DOREN, WHOSE TV CHEATING CAUSED A PUBLIC OUTRAGE.

MR. VAN D

AFTER PAINTING HIS VERMEER FAKES, HAN VAN MEEGEREN ROLLED THEM UP, CRACKING THE PAINT SO THAT THEY LOOKED AS OLD AS THE REAL MASTERPIECES.

Writing wrongs

Fakes are also common in the world of literature. The letters and notes of great authors fetch enormous prices. So forgers faithfully copy the paper, ink, and handwriting to make their work look authentic.

Fakespeares

This attention to detail is nothing new. When English forger William Ireland (1777–1835) taught himself to copy the writing style of William Shakespeare, he sliced pages out of 200-year-old legal papers. On them Ireland forged love letters and an I.O.U. by England's greatest playwright. Ireland's first attempts were harmless hoaxes made to please his father, a fan of Shakespeare. William would probably have got away with his crime if he had stopped there, but success made him bold. At the age of 19 he claimed to have "discovered" a new Shakespeare play: *Vortigern and Rowena*.

The news caused a stir. But when the play was performed, it was so bad that the audience laughed and booed. The show closed after the first night, and Ireland confessed that he had written it himself.

Though he later tried to earn a living as a respectable writer, nobody forgave Ireland's foolish childhood trick, and his work was never taken seriously.

Darwin's quest

As Ireland lay dying in 1835, English scientist Charles Darwin was figuring out an idea that would later inspire one of the most famous scientific forgeries in history.

In his theory of evolution, Darwin suggested that humans and apes might share the same ancestors. Now widely accepted, this idea seemed shocking at the time.

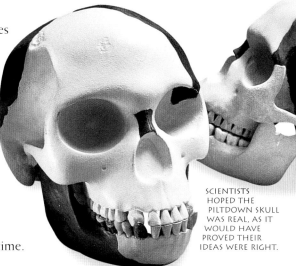

SCIENTISTS HOPED THE PILTDOWN SKULL WAS REAL, AS IT WOULD HAVE PROVED THEIR IDEAS WERE RIGHT.

THE APE'S TEETH HAD BEEN WORN AND STAINED TO APPEAR HUMAN

Fossil hunters scoured the world for bones that would prove Darwin right. Soon they had a chain of fossils (remains preserved in rock) stretching back to the most distant past. Together the fossils almost told the whole story. But a small gap still separated the remains of advanced apes from those of our primitive human ancestors.

The missing link
Then, in 1912, Charles Dawson, an amateur scientist, revealed an amazing discovery. Two years earlier at Piltdown Common, in southern England, he had dug up bits of a skull

and put them together. The skull looked human – but its jaw and teeth seemed ape-like.

Here was the "missing link", the proof everyone had been searching for! Unfortunately, Piltdown man was a forgery. Someone had cobbled together the skull of a modern man with the jaw of an orang-utan and a chimp's teeth. Modern tests showed up the hoax in 1953.

Who was the forger? Dawson is the key suspect, but he'd been dead a long time when the fake was exposed. There was a suggestion, in 1983, that Arthur Conan Doyle, author of the Sherlock Holmes stories, was involved. This might seem incredible, but Doyle's name was linked with another famous fraud in 1917.

Fairy tale

The "Cottingley fairies" were dreamed up by two imaginative schoolgirls from the village of Cottingley, in northern England. Elsie Wright and her cousin Frances Griffiths claimed they had fairies living at the bottom of their garden, and used a simple camera to photograph them.

Their families laughed at the pictures until the girls' mothers heard a lecture on theosophy, a religion that encourages belief in spirits. Theosophists were eager to believe that the pictures were genuine. When Conan Doyle saw them, he was convinced they weren't fakes.

Elsie and Frances hadn't really photographed fairies. They'd simpy cut pictures out of books and pinned them up in the woodland scene. But their hoax was just a little bit too clever. The attention the photographs attracted made it hard for them to admit what they had done. They were so ashamed of their fraud that they didn't tell the truth for nearly 60 years.

LOG ON...
www.pbs.org/wgbh/amex/quizshow/people events/pande02.html

THE COTTINGLEY "FAIRIES" NOW LOOK SO OBVIOUSLY FAKED THAT IT'S DIFFICULT TO BELIEVE SO MANY PEOPLE WERE FOOLED.

TRAITORS AND SPIES

Can you keep a secret? Of course you can! But what if someone else wants to know it, and offers you anything you ask for in exchange? Revealing the secret makes you a traitor – someone who at first seems to be trustworthy, but later betrays their friends or country. Spies are professional traitors. They collect the secrets of one country to sell to another.

Kiss of death

The most famous traitor of all lived about 2,000 years ago. He was Judas Iscariot, one of the 12 trusted disciples of Jesus Christ. In exchange for 30 pieces of silver, Judas offered to identify Jesus, who had angered

BONFIRES ON NOVEMBER 5 MARK THE FAILED GUNPOWDER PLOT

priests by claiming to be God's son. Jesus, greeted with a kiss from Judas, was arrested by the Romans and put to death.

Gunpowder, treason, and plot

Judas' crime was to betray a friend, but many more traitors are famous for betraying their countries. One of them, Guy Fawkes, caused so much hatred that English people still burn models of him ("guys") each year. Guy Fawkes (1570–1606) was a member of a group of Catholics who

GUY FAWKES (IN RED) USUALLY TAKES THE BLAME FOR THE GUNPOWDER PLOT, BUT ROBERT CATESBY (RIGHT) LED IT.

IN BRITAIN, FIREWORKS ARE A COLOURFUL AND NOISY REMINDER OF GUY FAWKES AND HIS TREASONOUS PLOT.

were angry with England's Protestant king, James I. They didn't think he was doing enough to protect Catholics. In protest, they planned to blow up England's Parliament building on 5 November 1605, when it would have been filled with politicians – and the king.

The plotters persuaded Fawkes to join them. As a soldier, he knew about explosives, and because he was not as well known as the others, he could move around without being recognized.

The gang rented a room under Parliament and packed it with gunpowder. But news of the plan had leaked out, and

69

THE AMERICANS HANGED
JOHN ANDRÉ, WHO TOOK
THE BLAME FOR BEN
ARNOLD'S TREACHERY.

suggests that traitors are generally hated whichever side they are on.

Traitor to the cause Benedict Arnold (1741–1801) was an outstanding American army officer when the War of Independence began in 1775. Arnold was a patriot. Like most Americans, he wanted to end British rule of his country. But other officers saw him as impatient and foolish. When they were promoted above him, Arnold grew angry and bitter. Placed in charge of the city of Philadelphia, he mixed with loyalists – Americans who wanted British rule to continue. He copied their wasteful lifestyle, and got into debt. Impressed by their views, he secretly decided to change sides.

WEIRD WORLD

IN THE UNITED STATES A "BENEDICT ARNOLD" IS STILL A NICKNAME FOR A TRAITOR. IN ENGLAND, IT'S THE NAME OF A KIND OF OMELETTE.

guards caught Fawkes red-handed in the room. Under pain of torture, he gave away the names of the other plotters. Most, including Fawkes, were executed.

Fawkes expected to become a hero if his traitorous acts had succeeded, but he might well have been disappointed. The story of an American spy

Arnold's dirty deal

When he was put in command of West Point, an important American fort, Arnold saw a way to pay off his debts while helping the British win the war. He offered to surrender the fort for £20,000, and arranged a secret midnight meeting to complete the deal with a British officer, Major John André.

Through a series of blunders and coincidences, André fell into the Americans' hands. Though they discovered Arnold's plan, it was too late to stop him from escaping – leaving John André to take the blame.

Hated for his treachery in America, Arnold fled to England. But his disloyalty to his country – and to André, who was executed – made him an outcast even in London, where he died penniless.

Deadly beauty

Like Arnold, the female spy Mata Hari worked for both sides in a war. In World War I (1914–18) the nations of Europe fought for control of the continent.

Mata Hari, a beautiful dancer, charmed both German officers and their French enemies. At least one man, a German officer, became a close friend and gave her money.

Later on in the war, Mata Hari agreed to spy for the French, but did not tell them about her special German friend and his presents. Her spymasters grew suspicious, though, and arrested her.

At the trial, nobody could prove that Mata Hari had sold French secrets. But the fact that she had received gifts of money

LOG ON...
Find out more on
www.bonefire.org/guy/

MATA HARI POSED AS A DANCER FROM JAVA, BUT THE TRUTH WAS MUCH LESS EXCITING – SHE WAS A DUTCH HOUSEWIFE.

convinced the court she was guilty. The dancer was shot as a spy in 1917.

S py versus spy

Mata Hari was a victim of the fierce loyalty that people feel for their country during wartime. Often these passionate feelings continue when peace returns.

After World War II (1939–45), for example, the USA and Russia were locked in rivalry. Though these two "super-powers" never actually fought, each built ever-bigger nuclear weapons to defend themselves. In this hostile atmosphere, nicknamed the Cold War, spies from both sides tried to find the secrets of their enemy's atom bombs.

D ouble trouble

A few spies played a deadly game. They pretended to work for one side, while actually sending secrets to the other. Known as double agents, they were hated villains in the country they spied on. But they were heroes in the nation they really served.
The identity of genuine double agents was secret, but books and films gave a taste of the exciting world in which Cold War spies operated.
The most famous were Ian Fleming's tales of James Bond. In these stories, dashing

SEAN CONNERY PLAYED THE SMOOTH SECRET AGENT 007 IN DOCTOR NO, THE FIRST OF 20 BOND MOVIES.

secret agent 007 uses all kinds of tricks and gadgets to outwit rival spies and other villains.

S pies' toys

Fleming based characters in the books on his wartime experiences with Britain's Secret Intelligence Service. "Q", for example, who builds Bond's ingenious and tiny gadgets in the books, was a real-life inventor, Charles Fraser Smith (1904–92).

BODY OF PEN HAS BEEN CUT AWAY TO SHOW TRANSMITTER INSIDE

TUBE HOUSES BATTERY WITH ENOUGH POWER FOR UP TO SIX HOURS

TODAY'S SPIES REALLY USE 007 GADGETS – THIS BUGGED PEN BROADCASTS CONVERSATIONS WITH A RADIO TRANSMITTER

BOND CREATOR IAN FLEMING HAD A PEN THAT FIRED TEAR GAS

For 007, Fleming used himself as a model. The author spent the war safe in a London office, but he longed for the excitement and danger of real spying. Only in his books could he slay evil foes, save the world from destruction, then calmly stroll to the bar and order a cocktail … "Shaken, not stirred".

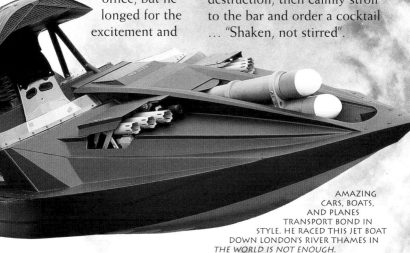

AMAZING CARS, BOATS, AND PLANES TRANSPORT BOND IN STYLE. HE RACED THIS JET BOAT DOWN LONDON'S RIVER THAMES IN *THE WORLD IS NOT ENOUGH*.

TERRIBLE TYRANTS

Nobody is more dangerous and terrible than a wicked ruler. Evil emperors, kings, and queens once had total power over those they governed – and all too often, the power went to their heads. At their command whole cities were destroyed and their people horribly murdered. Today, a few dictators have similar power. They use it for their cruel pleasure, to make themselves rich, or to gain still more power.

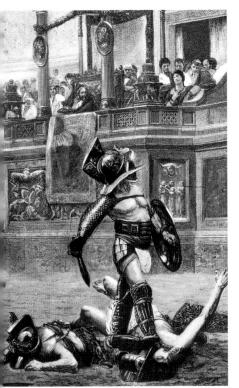

CRUELTY WAS POPULAR IN NERO'S ROME. FANS CHEERED GLADIATORS' DEATH-FIGHTS JUST AS WE CHEER FOOTBALL MATCHES.

The mad and bad

Ancient Rome's emperors were famous for their tyranny (abuse of limitless power). From their capital city in Italy, they ruled a vast empire in Europe and around the Mediterranean Sea. Booty from conquered lands made them rich, while Rome's laws allowed them to do almost anything they pleased.

Cruel Caligula

Emperor Caligula (AD 12–41) never let anyone forget this fact. He even reminded his wife that "… off comes this beautiful head, whenever I give the word".

Not that a reminder was necessary, for Caligula was well known for his cruelty. He took a horrible delight in tormenting his victims, and in watching them die a lingering death.

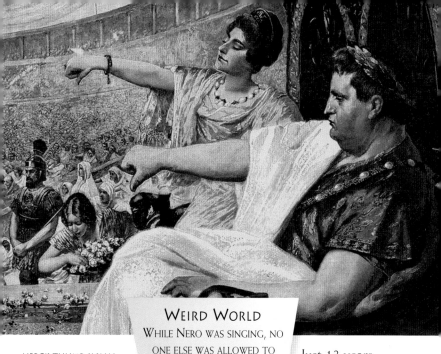

NERO'S THUMB SIGNAL MEANT DEATH FOR DEFEATED GLADIATORS.

WEIRD WORLD
WHILE NERO WAS SINGING, NO ONE ELSE WAS ALLOWED TO LEAVE THE THEATRE. SOME WOULD LEAP FROM THE WALLS OR FEIGN DEATH.

Caligula was also a big spender. In one year he spent a sum equal to 1.8 *million* times the annual pay of a soldier. Then he forced wealthy Romans to pay for his lavish lifestyle.

Mental illness may have been the cause of Caligula's wicked ways, and his madness grew as he aged. In AD 40 he marched troops north to invade Britain. But at the coast he told them to stop and collect sea shells.

Spoiled brat

The very next year, Caligula was murdered – but another mad leader soon took his place.

Just 13 years later, Caligula's grand-nephew Nero (AD 37–68) became emperor.

As a young man Nero liked to play silly pranks, but like his great-uncle Caligula he grew up to be very strange. When competing in musical competitions, chariot races, and plays, he demanded first prize – even though other contestants were much better.

Nero began to use his power in cruel ways. When his mother told him off, he had her murdered. When he tired of his wife, she was killed, too.

Nero's vanity, cruelty, and greed made him widely hated, and by AD 68 even his friends

VLAD DRACOLYA CALMLY SAT DOWN TO DINNER WHILE HIS VICTIMS WERE IMPALED ON STAKES AND THEN BUTCHERED.

had left him. Though he fled Rome, Nero was captured and executed like a slave – tied to a cross and whipped to death.

Vlad the Impaler

Nero's cruelty takes some beating, but Vlad Dracolya (1431–76) had a try. Vlad was a prince from Walachia. Now part of Romania, Walachia lay on a main route to Asia and had a long history of

GERMAN MONKS FLEEING VLADS CRUEL TYRANNY SPREAD BLOOD-DRINKING RUMOURS THAT GREW INTO THE VAMPIRE LEGEND.

invasion. Vlad himself was imprisoned by Turkish conquerors.

On his release, Vlad was determined to free his country from foreign rule, and began by getting rid of those he did not trust. He enslaved treacherous nobles and forced them to build a castle. The old and weak he had skewered on wooden stakes, earning the nickname "Vlad the Impaler." He once ordered guards to nail a guest's turban to his head because he would not remove it.

In his six-year reign, Vlad may have killed as many as 100,000 people. It's hardly surprising, then, that his name itself became a gory legend. Writer Bram Stoker made him the blood-drinking vampire of his horror novel *Dracula* (1897).

Tyrannical Cesare

In the year that Vlad died, a boy was born in Italy who would grow up to be one of that country's greatest tyrants.

Cesare Borgia (1476?–1507) was the son of a corrupt Pope (bishop of Rome). With the help of his father and ruthless sister Lucrezia, Cesare used murder and treachery to acquire enormous power.

THE BORGIAS' BANQUET GUESTS AVOIDED POISONING BY BRINGING THEIR OWN WINE AND POURING IT THEMSELVES.

Cesare's aim was to turn the rich lands of central Italy into his own mini-empire. To do this, he used warfare, cheating, scheming, and treachery. All politicians of the time used dirty tricks, but none so expertly as Cesare. He used a professional poisoner and a strangler to despatch enemies. These were secret ways of death, but Cesare also knew the terror value of public killing. He once left a victim's body in a city square, together with the axe that had hacked it to bits.

When his father died in 1503, Cesare's luck finally ran out. His rivals grabbed power and threw him in prison.

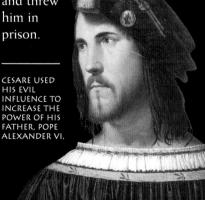

CESARE USED HIS EVIL INFLUENCE TO INCREASE THE POWER OF HIS FATHER, POPE ALEXANDER VI.

Cesare managed to escape, only to die fighting as a soldier-for-hire in Spain.

Ivan the Terrible

Cesare's motto was "Either Caesar or Nothing". Like the Roman emperors he was named after, he wanted total power. The word Caesar gave Russians a name for their emperors, the "czars" or "tsars". The first to officially hold this title was Czar Ivan IV (1530–84). History remembers him by a different name: Ivan the Terrible.

Ivan earned his nickname after losing a war against neighbouring Livonia (now Estonia and Latvia). Russia's warrior-noblemen, the boyars, betrayed him during the war, and he was determined to get his revenge.

Assembling a huge private army, Ivan set off in 1570 for Novgorod, a stronghold of his enemies. His revenge was swift, cruel, and bloody. The day after arriving in the city he announced that a thousand people a day would be tortured to death in front of him and his son.

IVAN THE TERRIBLE (PLAYED HERE BY A FILM ACTOR) HAD A MAGNIFICENT CATHEDRAL BUILT IN MOSCOW TO CELEBRATE HIS WAR VICTORIES.

LOG ON...
www.roman-emperors.org/gaius.htm

ROBESPIERRE, SHOWN HERE AS EXECUTIONER, DID NOT REGRET SENDING SO MANY PEOPLE TO THE GUILLOTINE. "PITY IS TREASON," HE SAID.

When the revolution broke out in 1789, peasant people all over France rose up against the nobles. They wanted social justice and an end to poverty. But by 1793 the revolt was descending into chaos.

To put the revolution back on track, Robespierre began what was called the Reign of Terror – 10 months of executions. At first, only the corrupt rich lost their heads. But Robespierre could not control the movement he had started. Soon, nobody was safe, and about 17,000 people went to the guillotine.

By mid-1794 Robespierre had lost popular support, and he finally fell victim to the blade that had killed so many.

WEIRD WORLD
THE GUILLOTINE'S INVENTOR CLAIMED VICTIMS FELT ONLY "A SLIGHT CHILL ON THE NECK" AS THE BLADE SLICED OFF THEIR HEADS.

He kept his word. In the next five weeks up to 60,000 people died. Some were slowly roasted, or pushed through ice on the river. Ivan devised ever more beastly deaths for the rest.

Reign of Terror
The victims of French tyrant Maximilien Robespierre (1758–94) were spared such agonies. They died quickly on the guillotine, a new beheading machine specially invented to execute nobles during the French Revolution.

Today, bloody uprisings like the French Revolution are a stern reminder to rulers that cruelty doesn't pay. Sadly, there are usually plenty of vile tyrants waiting to take over as soon as the last one is booted from power.

ARCHVILLAINS

They are powerful, cunning, and deadly – yet nobody knows them. Masterminds of the criminal underworld, they direct armies of villains to commit dark deeds. Whatever villainy they organize, it cannot be

traced back to them. These evil geniuses are sometimes called archvillains – leaders of villains. Like the shadows of night, they are magnified by our imagination into something truly frightening.

"GOODBYE MR BOND!" SNEERS EVIL ARCHVILLAIN BLOFELD, BEFORE SENDING 007 ON HIS WAY TO A PAINFUL AND ORIGINAL DEATH.

Supreme evil
Their power to create fear has made criminal geniuses favourite characters for mystery and crime writers. In the famous spy movies, for instance, James Bond's toughest foe is evil crime-lord Ernst Stavro Blofeld.

WEIRD WORLD
ACTOR DONALD PLEASENCE TRIED HUMPS, LAME HANDS, AND BEARDS TO MAKE BLOFELD MORE SINISTER, BEFORE SETTLING ON SCAR MAKE-UP.

In the early films, cinema audiences saw only his hands stroking a white cat. Then, in *You Only Live Twice* (1967), 007 met his arch-enemy face to face. The sinister mastermind character reappeared as Dr Evil in the Bond spoof *Austin Powers: International Man of Mystery*. Preserved in ice for 30 years,

Dr Evil thaws out to pit his wits against a secret agent stuck in the same sixties time warp.

Adam Worth

Of course, Doctor Evil and Blofeld are just imaginary figures, created to scare us or amuse us – aren't they?

Wrong. Criminal masterminds really do exist. One of the cleverest was an American, Adam Worth (1844–1902). He started out organizing the petty thieves of Manhattan in New York.

In 1869 he pulled off a daring robbery. By drilling through a wall he stole a million dollars from a bank vault. When detectives from the famous Pinkerton's agency got on his trail, Worth fled to Europe.

High life, low life

Worth bought a mansion in leafy south London, and a townhouse in fashionable

IN HIS SECOND OUTING AS AUSTIN POWERS' ARCH-ENEMY, DR EVIL IS JOINED BY A PINT-SIZED SIDE-KICK, MINI-ME.

Mayfair became the centre of his crime empire. He planned "check-forging, swindling, safe-cracking, diamond robbery, burglary of every degree, and bank robbery ...", according to Pinkerton's. Worth set up the crimes, and raked in the profits, but rarely took part in them. The villains who stole for him didn't even know who gave them their orders.

But Worth's boldest crime he carried out himself. One night in May 1876 he forced open the window of a London art gallery. From

TO STEAL PRECIOUS GEMS FROM SOUTH AFRICA, ADAM WORTH DISGUISED HIMSELF AS AN OSTRICH FEATHER DEALER.

Worth's downfall came through a foolish mistake. Caught during a bungled bank raid in Belgium, he was arrested and jailed for seven years.

Criminal genius

Worth died five years after his release, but his spirit lived on – in the stories of detective Sherlock Holmes.

In 1893 their author, Arthur Conan Doyle, used Worth as the model for the evil archvillain Professor James Moriarty. As Holmes explains to his faithful companion Dr Watson, Moriarty is "a genius .... He does little

under the nose of a sleeping watchman he stole the most valuable portrait ever, a work by the artist Thomas

WAS RASPUTIN A FAITH HEALER OR AN EVIL FRAUD?

Gainsborough. Four years later Worth pulled off an even more spectacular robbery, stealing diamonds worth $500,000.

More than 12 years of respectability and wealth followed, as Worth settled in to the double life of a gentleman criminal. By day he was a rich playboy. By night he organized half of London's crime.

himself. He only plans. But his agents are numerous and splendidly organized."

Moriarty's first appearance in print, in the short story "The Final Problem", was meant to be Holmes' last. Both men vanish in a fight on a mountain in Europe (though Conan Doyle later wrote more stories in which the two battle).

Getting rid of a story-book villain takes a sentence or two. Eliminating a real one is harder, as the assassins of Russian "mad monk" Rasputin discovered.

Unholy schemer

Born in Siberia in about 1871, Grigory Yefimovich Novykh studied as a monk, and later became a wandering holy man. Rumours spread that he could heal the sick and predict the future. But his filthy clothing and revolting manners soon earned him the nickname Rasputin, which roughly translated means "slob".

Rasputin visited Russia's capital, St Petersburg. This is where he met the Russian czar (emperor) Nicholas, his wife Alexandra, and their sick son Alexei. The smelly stranger with staring eyes was welcomed at the imperial court. By using his healing ability to make the boy well, Rasputin gained power over the royal family.

Abuse of power

Rasputin wielded power ruthlessly, giving friends good jobs in the church and government. By 1916 it was clear that Rasputin's influence was causing Russia great harm.

So on a freezing December night his enemies fed him poisoned wine and cakes. The poison – enough to kill a horse

RASPUTIN TOLD HIS FOLLOWERS THAT UNLESS THEY JOINED HIM IN SINNING, THEY COULD NOT REGRET THEIR SINS AND BE FORGIVEN BY GOD.

– hardly affected Rasputin, so the plotters beat him and shot him. Even bullets would not kill him. Only when the murderers threw him from a bridge into the frozen River Neva did Rasputin die.

Mr Big

While Rasputin was controlling the Russian imperial court, an archvillain of another sort had risen to power on the other side of the world. Arnold Rothstein (1882–1928) was perhaps the most powerful man in New York – but he had not been elected. He was responsible for countless crimes – but was never tried for any of them.

Rothstein was a criminal mastermind like no other. He was a mathematical wizard, and as a teenager he used his ability to calculate gambling odds (the chances of success). His wins made him rich. When alcohol was banned in the United States in 1920, Rothstein backed the gangsters who supplied it illegally.

Rothstein was wise enough to ensure none of the crimes he fixed could be traced to him.

The closest he ever got to trouble was a 1919 enquiry into baseball's World Series. Rothstein had fixed the game, bribing eight members of the Chicago team to deliberately lose. The eight players were arrested – but before the trial, vital evidence mysteriously vanished from police files.

When questioned, Rothstein acted innocent. "A gang of thugs bar my path," he said, "...as if I was a notorious person, a criminal even!"

Of course he was a criminal, and in 1928 New York's violent underworld caught up with him. After refusing to pay his losses in a two-day-long card game, Arnold Rothstein, or "The Big Bankroll", or "Mr Big", was shot dead.

ARNOLD ROTHSTEIN BET HEAVILY THAT THE CINCINNATI REDS WOULD WIN THE 1919 BASEBALL WORLD SERIES – THEN BRIBED THEIR CHICAGO RIVALS TO LOSE.

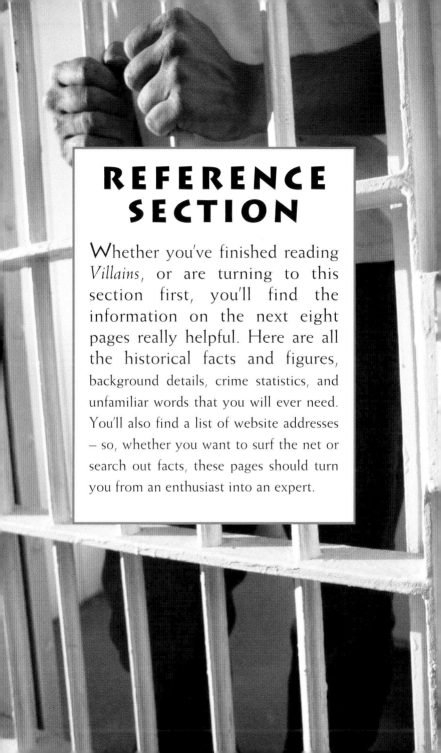

REFERENCE SECTION

Whether you've finished reading *Villains*, or are turning to this section first, you'll find the information on the next eight pages really helpful. Here are all the historical facts and figures, background details, crime statistics, and unfamiliar words that you will ever need. You'll also find a list of website addresses – so, whether you want to surf the net or search out facts, these pages should turn you from an enthusiast into an expert.

VILLAINS THROUGH HISTORY

AD 30 approx. Palestinian disciple (follower) Judas Iscariot betrayed his master, Jesus Christ, leading to Christ's death by crucifixion.

AD 37 Roman nobleman Caligula (AD 12–41) became emperor. He was known for his cruelty.

AD 65 Vain, extravagant Roman emperor Nero (AD 37–68) started to build himself a vast palace after fire destroyed half of Rome.

1457 Romanian prince Vlad Dracolya (1431–76) began attacks on his country's noblemen, earning him the nickname "the Impaler".

1503 The power of much-feared Italian prince Cesare Borgia (1476?–1507) started to crumble after his father, the Pope, died.

1570 For his torture and murder of his foes in Novgorod, Russian Czar Ivan IV (1530–84) was nicknamed "Ivan the Terrible".

1572 Sailor Francis Drake (1540?–96) began raids in the Caribbean, where European powers had established trading colonies. His exploits made him famous as a pirate in Spain and as a hero in his native England.

1605 English soldier Guy Fawkes (1570–1606) was caught making a huge bomb under England's Parliament building.

1659 London's famous pickpocket and highwaywoman Moll Cutpurse

(alias Mary Frith b.1589) died.

1666 English newspapers reported the first hold-ups by Claud Duval (1643–70), a French highwayman known for his charm.

1671 Irish rebel Colonel Thomas Blood (c.1618–80) nearly succeeded in a cunning plan to steal England's Crown Jewels.

1676 English highwayman William Nevison (1639–85) made an epic ride to avoid accusations of robbery.

1718 The short career of fearsome English pirate Blackbeard (real name Edward Teach) ended in a fight to the death with the English navy.

1720 Fearless British pirates Mary Read (1690–1720) and Anne Bonny were captured and tried, but escaped execution by claiming that they were both pregnant.

1721 Welsh sailor Bartholomew "Black Bart" Roberts (1682–1722) began raids on ships in the Indian Ocean which would make him the most successful pirate of all time.

1737 Dashing English highwayman Dick Turpin (1705–39) hid in a cave near London to escape capture.

1775–83 Citizens of England's American colonies fought a revolutionary War of Independence for the right to rule themselves. In 1779 American traitor Benedict Arnold (1741–1801) offered to surrender his fort to the English.

1779 From his *Temple of Health* Scots doctor James Graham (1745–94) sold bogus cures to London's rich.

1789–99 In a bloody revolution ordinary people seized power from the noble families who ruled France. In 1794 the revolutionaries turned against their leader Maximilien Robespierre (1758–94) and executed him on the guillotine.

1825 The grisly English legend of Sweeney Todd began with a story of a pie-making killer barber in *Tell-Tale Magazine*.

1828 Irish murderers William Burke (1792–1829) and William Hare (1790–1860) sold their victims' bodies to surgeons in Edinburgh.

1861–65 In a civil war over slavery, Northern American states fought and beat the Southern states. In 1865, to avenge the South's defeat, failed American actor John Wilkes Booth (1839–65) shot and killed president Abraham Lincoln.

1868 Ruthless, racist Wild-West gunman John Wesley Hardin (1853–95) shot his first victim.

1873 The James brothers, Jesse (1847–82) and Frank (1843–1915) led their famous bandit gang in their first train robbery.

1876 American archvillain Adam Worth (1844–1902) stole a famous Gainsborough portrait of the Duchess of Devonshire.

1880 English card-sharp "Canada" Bill Jones died in the USA after a lifetime swindling "suckers".

1880 Police marksmen shot down Australian bushranger Ned Kelly despite his home-made armour. Kelly was executed later that year.

1881 Young gunfighter Billy the Kid (born Henry McCarty 1859/60–1881) was ambushed and shot dead by lawman Pat Garrett.

1888 "Jack the Ripper" killed and carved up seven London women, but escaped capture.

1890 Failed US doctor Herman Webster Mudgett (1860–96) built the mansion where he would allegedly kill more than 100 people.

1893 A US court found Lizzie Borden (1860–1927) not guilty of killing her parents with an axe.

1896 American outlaw Butch Cassidy (alias Robert Leroy Parker, 1866–1909?) formed the Wild Bunch, a collection of train robbers.

1903 Quick-tempered outlaw and Wild Bunch member Kid Curry (alias Harvey Logan 1865–1903) escaped from jail.

1908 Siberian monk Grigory Rasputin (1871–1916) healed the sick son of the Russian czar and gained power over the royal family.

1909 Bolivian soldiers killed the Sundance Kid (alias Harry Longabaugh 1870–1909), the best gunman of the Wild Bunch.

1910 American poisoner Dr Hawley Crippen (1862–1910) was captured thanks to the newly invented radio as he fled to Canada.

1910–12 English amateur scientist Charles Dawson (1846–1916) faked fossil finds to prove the theory of evolution.

1914 Bosnian agitator Gavrilo Princip (1894–1918) assassinated an Austrian nobleman. The shooting triggered World War I (1914–18), in which millions died.

1917 Dutch exotic dancer Mata Hari (alias Margaretha Macleod 1876–1917) was shot as a spy.

1917 English schoolgirls Elsie Wright (b.1901) and Frances Griffiths (b.1907) fooled the famous with fake fairy photos.

1919 Prohibition (a ban on alcohol) in the USA led to a huge growth in organized crime.

1920 US gambling tycoon Arnold Rothstein (1882–1928) denied bribing baseball players to fix the 1919 World Series.

1920 Thousands of Americans lost their savings as a "pyramid scheme" run by Italian-born Charles Ponzi (c.1882–1949) collapsed.

1920s American con man Joseph Weil (1875–1976) sold worthless land to Chicago citizens in cunning real-estate swindles.

1929 Hoodlum Al "Scarface" Capone (1899–1947) terrorized his rivals with machine-gun shoot-outs to become crime boss of Chicago.

1934 Small-time robbers Bonnie Parker (b.1911) and Clyde Barrow (b.1909) were shot dead in a police ambush after a year-long hunt.

1934 American bank robber John Dillinger (1903–34) broke out of gaol armed with a carved wooden gun.

1944 American organized crime boss Louis Buchalter (alias Lepke 1897–1944) was executed for his leadership of the "gun-for-hire" company Murder, Inc. His partner, Italian-American Albert Anastasia (alias Umberto Anastasio 1902–57) continued the business.

1945 Dutch painter Han Van Meegeren (1889–1947) admitted faking valuable "old" paintings which fooled many museum experts.

1946 Japanese gangster Kazuo "The Bear" Taoka (1912–81) became leader of a yakuza (organized crime) group. He went on to became Japan's most powerful crime boss.

1953 Julius (b.1918) and Ethel (b.1915) Rosenberg became the only American civilians to be executed for spying.

1956 American university professor Charles van Doren (b. 1926) cheated his way to success in the television quiz show *Twenty One*.

1976 French robber Albert Spaggiari (b. 1932) escaped with a fortune in gold after tunnelling into a Nice bank vault from the sewers.

1983 India's "bandit queen" Phoolan Devi (1957–2001) was jailed for the revenge murder of 20 men who humiliated her, but became a folk hero on her release in 1994.

CRIMINAL RECORDS

Comparing crimes is not easy because the value of money changes. This selective list shows some of the biggest thefts in recent times, with their estimated present-day value.

Greediest tyrant
1966–86, at least £1 billion
While Ferdinand Marcos was president of the Philippines, he and his wife Imelda stole more than £1 billion from the people they ruled. Imelda used some of her fortune to buy shoes – she had an estimated 300 pairs.

Biggest mugging
1990, £400 million
On 2 May 1990 John Goddard, a banker's messenger, was robbed at knifepoint in a London street. The bonds (valuable bank certificates) he was carrying were worth £292 million at the time.

Greatest art theft
1990, £227 million
Thieves dressed as policemen broke into Boston's Isabella Stewart Gardner Museum on 18 March 1990. They escaped with 13 valuable paintings by artists Rembrandt, Manet, Degas, and Vermeer.

Biggest bank bust
1976, £100 million
Thieves in Lebanon blasted their way into the British Bank of the Middle East from the church next door in January 1976. They cracked the safe and stole the contents of private safe-deposit boxes. The booty weighed so much that the thieves drove it away in lorries.

Sparkling jewel robbery
1994, £36 million
Three robbers firing guns held up a jewellery store at the Carlton Hotel in Cannes, France, on 11 August 1994, taking jewellery worth 250 million French francs. Police discovered after the robbery that guns had been loaded with blanks.

Great Train Robbery
1963, £32 million
In Britain's most famous theft, thieves stopped a mail train in August 1963 and unloaded mail-bags containing used banknotes. When caught, the thieves were sentenced to a total of 300 years in jail.

Weighty gold bars
1983, £32 million
London's Heathrow airport was the scene of the biggest gold robbery of all time when thieves took 6,800 bars, packed in 76 cardboard boxes, from the Brinks Mat warehouse.

Vast computer bank fraud
1994, £7.8 million
Russian student Vladimir Levin used a laptop computer in his St Petersburg apartment to hack into the network of Citibank and electronically transfer $10 million dollars into his bank account and those of his friends.

FIGHTING CRIME

The first modern police force was set up in Paris, France, in 1667. The forces of most English-speaking countries are based on London's Metropolitan Police.

BRITAIN
Metropolitan Police
The "bobbies" of the Met are named after Robert Peel, who founded London's police force in 1829.
History: www.met.police.uk/history/crime_museum.htm

Special Branch
A division of the Met, Special Branch fights terrorism and political crime, and protects politicians.

MI5, MI6
Britain has two security intelligence (spy) agencies. MI5 operates within Britain to catch spies and terrorists, and to help the police fight serious crime. MI6 is the British Secret Service, sending British spies abroad.
Homepage: www.mi5.gov.uk/

FRANCE
National Gendarmerie, National Police
France has two police forces. Army soldiers make up the National Gendarmerie. The National Police, France's main crime-fighting force, was formed in 1966.

UNITED STATES
Federal Bureau of Investigation
America's national police force, the FBI, investigates certain serious crimes, and provides other police forces with training, laboratories, and data.

Secret Service
America's Secret Service was started in 1865 to try and stop forgers from printing counterfeit money. After the 1901 assassination of President McKinley, it took on another job – guarding the president.
Home page: www.fbi.gov/kids/k5th/kidsk5th.htm

Central Intelligence Agency
The CIA's main work is to study all kinds of information, gathered from all over the world, and use it to advise political leaders.
Kids' page:
www.cia.gov/cia/ciakids/index.html

Pinkertons
The private detective agency founded by Scottish immigrant Allan Pinkerton in 1850 grew into one of the most important American crime-fighting organizations.
Homepage:
www.pinkertons.com/companyinfo/history/pinkerton/index.asp

INTERNATIONAL
Interpol
The world's police forces share information through Interpol, the International Criminal Police Organization. Interpol was founded in 1923, and today more than 125 countries take part.
Homepage: http://www.interpol.int/

PUNISHMENT

If villains are captured, they go to court for a trial. This is a test that decides whether they are guilty of (responsible for) the crimes of which they are accused. If the court decides a villain is guilty, the judge sets the punishment. In the past there were many different kinds of punishment. Some were very cruel.

Corporal punishment

One of the oldest penalties for crime is corporal punishment – pain or injury to the body. Villains could be whipped, branded (burned with a hot iron), or blinded, or they had part of their body cut off – an ear, a nose, a hand, or a foot. Whipping continued in England until 1967, and in the USA until 1952. It is still common in many countries.

Ordeals

In these old, cruel, and superstitious trials, people believed that God decided a villain's guilt. In ordeal by water a suspected criminal was thrown into a lake or river. Those who floated were judged guilty, but others drowned. Ordeal by cursed morsel involved eating things like feathers — innocent people choked.

Outlawry

Under English law, murderers had to pay compensation to the victim's family. Those who could not became outlaws – they were *outside* of the *law's* protection. They lost their possessions, and anyone could kill them.

Capital punishment

The ultimate punishment is the death penalty, or execution. Often called capital punishment, this ancient penalty is still widely used in China, Iran, Saudi Arabia, and the USA. About half the world's nations no longer use the death penalty because their people believe that it is too cruel to end human life, however great the crime.

Transportation

In England, those criminals spared execution were often transported – sent to punishment camps in Australia or North America. You could be transported for merely stealing a pig. Because of the cruel treatment the prisoners suffered, transportation ended in the 1850s.

Fines and reparation

Payment of money to a court (a fine) is an alternative to more brutal forms of punishment. Fines punish the poor more than the rich, so in some countries villains pay a number of day's wages, instead of a fixed sum of money.

Imprisonment

Locking villains up is a relatively new form of punishment. Prisons used to be a way of preventing people from escaping between capture and trial or punishment. Long-term imprisonment began in 19th-century Britain as a way of teaching villains to lead better lives while protecting society.

GLOSSARY

Alibi
A story that proves someone accused of a crime was elsewhere at the time.

Anarchy
A state of lawlessness in which crime can run riot. Often results from poor leadership of a country, or from revolution or civil war.

Arson
Deliberately starting fires.

Assassination
Killing for political reasons.

Blackmail
Threatening to reveal damaging information about someone unless they pay money.

Booty
Stolen property.

Bushranger
Australian highwayman or bandit.

Burglary
Stealing property from a building.

Capital punishment
see *death penalty*.

Card-sharp
Someone who makes their living cheating at cards.

Confidence trickster
Swindler who wins a victim's trust in order to cheat him or her.

Con man
see *confidence trickster*.

Corpse
A dead body.

Counterfeit
Faked – usually referring to money.

Death penalty
Punishment of a crime by killing the criminal.

Dictator
A leader with unlimited power.

Empire
A big organization ruled by a single person or family. Also a collection of several countries under a single nation or ruler.

Execution
Punishment killing.

Extortion
Using threats to demand money.

Felony
A crime regarded by the law as serious, usually involving violence.

Fingerprint
Traces of skin pattern left by touching something, used to help police identify villains.

Forced labour
Making prisoners work hard as a punishment.

Forgery
Copying something to sell as real.

Fraud
A dishonest way of making money.

Hanging
Punishment killing by strangulation with a rope.

Highwayman
A street robber who rides a horse.

Hoax
A cheat or trick.

In cold blood
In a calm and ruthless way.

Jolly Roger
Black-and-white flag flown by pirate ships.

Libel
Writing or printing a hurtful lie about someone. See also *slander*.

Mafia
Criminal organization that spread from Sicily to the USA.

Misdemeanour
A minor crime.
Outlaw
Someone accused of crimes who
flees to avoid punishment.
Pickpocket
Street thief who steals from pockets.
Pirate
Sea robber.
Quack
Doctor who sells worthless cures.
Revenge
Getting your own back at someone.
Revolution
The often violent overthrow of a
country's rulers.
Robber
Violent thief.
Safe-cracking
Opening a safe without the keys.
Slander
Telling a lie about someone which
harms or hurts them. See also *libel*.
Slave
A worker treated like an animal.

Spy
Someone who tries to discover the
secrets of another country or, for
example, a rival organization.
Strangle
To kill a person by squeezing their
neck or windpipe.
Telegraph
Old-fashioned signalling system
that sends letters in a code of
electric pulses.
Traitor
Trusted person who cheats their
friends or country.
Treachery
Breaking trust or giving away secrets
(see traitor).
Tyranny
The abuse of absolute power.
Vault
An underground safe.
Wager
A bet.
Witness
Someone who sees a crime.

WEBSITES

www.crimelibrary.com/
The Crime Library is an excellent place to start reading up on villains.
www.historybuff.com/library/refcrime.html
Reprints of historic newspaper stories on infamous criminals.
www.alcaponemuseum.com/
An interactive website on Chicago gangster Al Capone
www.museumofhoaxes.com/
A website devoted to hoaxes of all sorts.
www.sherlock-holmes.org/english.htm
Everything you ever wanted to know about Sherlock Holmes.
http://library.thinkquest.org/2760/homep.htm
This "Anatomy of a Murder" website explains the US criminal justice system.
http://crime.about.com/library/blfiles/bl1800s.htm
A look back at infamous criminals of the 19th century.

INDEX

CREDITS

Dorling Kindersley would like to thank: Chris Bernstein for the index.

The author and editor would like to thank: Fran Jones, Mike Marinacci, and Stefan Podhorodecki.

Additional photography by:
Max Alexander, Geoff Brightling, Jane Burton, Andy Crawford, Tina Chambers, Geoff Dann, Steve Gorton, Bob Langrish, David Murray, Julian Selmes, Karl Shane, and Jerry Young.